Biblical Pacifism

Biblical Pacifism

A Peace Church Perspective

Dale W. Brown

With a Foreword by
Richard Baggett Deats

BRETHREN PRESS
Elgin, Illinois

Biblical Pacifism: A Peace Church Perspective

BRETHREN PRESS, 1451 Dundee
Avenue, Elgin, IL 60120

Cover: *Peaceable Kingdom* © 1848 by Edward Hicks (1780-1849). Courtesy of The Pennsylvania Academy of The Fine Arts, Broad and Cherry Streets, Philadelphia, PA 19102

Designed by Kathy Kline

Unless otherwise noted, Scripture quotations are from the Revised Standard Version of the Bible, copyrighted 1946, 1952, 1971, 1973 by the National Council of Churches of Christ in the U.S.A., Division of Education and Ministry.

Library of Congress Cataloging in Publication Data

Brown, Dale W., 1926-
  Biblical pacifism.

  Bibliography: p.
  Includes index.
    1. Peace—Religious aspects—Christianity.
2. Pacifism—Religious aspects—Christianity.
3. Historic peace churches. I. Title.
BT736.4B73   1986   261.8'73   85-30636
ISBN 0-87178-108-5

Printed in the United States of America

Dedicated with Appreciation
to Quakers and Mennonites
Whose Participation in The New Call to Peacemaking
Greatly Inspired and Enriched
My Understanding of Peacemaking

Table of Contents

Foreword

The Significance of
the Historic Peace Churches

"The only people on earth who do not see Christ and
His teachings as nonviolent are Christians." Mohan-
das Gandhi

It is not hard to see why Gandhi made such an observation.
His experiences in South Africa and India were during the hey-
day of Western imperialism, an era in history when the "Christian" nations of the West had spread their rule around the world.
In the name of "Christian civilization" imperial armies and
navies had subjugated nations and tribes throughout Africa,
Asia, and the Americas. Christian missionaries from the West
benefited from the spread of empire, with the preaching of the
cross often taking place under the protection of the sword. Slaves
and opium, God, gold, and glory all seemed to be intermixed as
subject peoples experienced western colonialism and the religion
that accompanied it.

The brute force and violence that was part of this imperial
expansion dated back to the fourth century of the Christian era.
The Emperor Constantine's conversion to Christianity ushered
in the identification of church and state, the cross and the sword.
The early Church had refused to bow the knee to Caesar, and
Christians did not serve in the armed forces, choices that
brought in their wake persecution and martyrdom.

After Constantine, however, a dramatic shift began: the
church blessed the state, the state protected the church and the
armed forces were now comprised of Christians. The flags and
banners of state and church were unfurled together, and armies
marched under the insignia of the cross. In the name of Christ
Crusaders slaughtered the infidel and conquered heathen lands.
Inquisitors tortured heretics to save their immortal souls. Catho-

lic battled Protestant and Protestant fought Protestant, as Christian rulers sought to enforce particular creedal formulations and practices within each nation state. Religious wars were commonplace. In the modern era, global wars I and II pitted Christian lands against each other.

The widespread Christian sanction of violence and warfare was found not only in the state churches but across the whole range of denominations. Church/State alliance and the just war theory following from it were the underpinnings of such support of the barbarism of war. Even though war might be deplored in general, and pleas for peace sincerely invoked, in each particular war—for whatever cause and with whatever means used—national interest and princely appeal were able to line up Christians to follow their country's flag to war, blessing the cause and praying for victory, even as Christians on the opposite side did exactly the same.

And yet, if this was the predominant response of Christians to war, there was another tradition, one that held the way of the cross to reject the way of the sword. This other way placed love of the enemy, the stranger, and the forgotten at the very heart of the gospel. Jesus was followed as the Prince of Peace who calls his disciples to be peacemakers. While this understanding was prevalent in the early church, after Constantine it increasingly became a minority position, seen for example in some of the monastic orders. It should also be noted that the church did attempt to limit war and to lay down certain codes of conduct for wartime.

When Protestantism burst upon the scene, the reformers attempted to purify the church and recapture the spirit and practice of the early Christians. Nonetheless, reformers such as Luther and Calvin continued in varying degrees the church/state alliance. They not only retained the just war theory; they gave it creedal status as well. "Christian" warfare not only continued unabated, but the breakup of the church and the rise of nationalism brought about its increase.

It was left to the radical wing of the Reformation to seriously challenge the state's co-opting of the Church, as seen most blatantly in the practice of warfare and other forms of violence that Christendom had come to accept as a necessary evil in a fallen world. There were especially three strands in this Reformation. In the sixteenth century, the Mennonites arose out of the Anabaptist wing Radical Reformation. In the seventeenth century the Society of Friends, or Quakers, came out of Radical Puritanism. and in the eighteenth century, the Brethren sprang from Radical Pietism.

Although there were distinctive differences between these groups then and now, together they constituted a radical understanding of the gospel that sharply broke with the traditional accommodation of the church to the demands of the state. This break was seen most clearly in their rejection of warfare and other forms of coercion, but it needs to be stressed that this rejection arose out of an understanding of the Christian community as having an integrity and calling apart from wider society. Furthermore, it expressed an allegiance transcending any particular tribal or national boundary and rule. The state and church were and are not the same. The church's calling is to the agape community.

It is out of such an understanding and commitment that biblical pacifism arises. It is a recovery of a central aspect of the gospel that had been lost (or relegated to convent and monastery). It was expressed in bold strokes by an early Quaker writer, Robert Barclay, who wrote in 1676:

> Whoever can reconcile this, "Resist not evil," with "Resist evil by force"; again, "Give also thy other cheek," with "Spoil them, make a prey of them, pursue them with fire and sword"; or "Pray for those that persecute you," with "Persecute them by fines, imprisonment, and death itself." Whoever can find a means to reconcile those things, may be supposed also to have found a way to reconcile God with the Devil, Christ with Anti-Christ, light with darkness, and good with evil.

This squarely biblical pacifism was at the heart of the radical witness of Mennonites, Quakers, and Brethren. This peace testimony not only brought them suffering at the hands of the state but by other churches as well. In standing apart from accepted practices and interpretations, they were often looked upon as heretics and traitors. Nonetheless, their testimony continued as a constant, if minority, witness. This witness they bore separately, as well as together on occasion. In the New World the three denominations found grounds for common witness in the Quaker-founded colony of Pennsylvania. There they treated the native Americans with fairness, respect, and assistance and they were recognized by the Indians as sharing a kinship that evoked trust and goodwill. While other colonists went to war with these so-called "savages", the pacifist Christians were able to live side by side with America's original inhabitants. They did not look for ways to wage a just war with the Indians because they practiced a just peace. In the Revolutionary War, and the Civil War a century later, the peace churches continued their peace testimony even in the face of derision and imprisonment.

At their best the peace churches did not merely seek exemption from military service for their own. They bore a positive witness of service and healing that bound up the broken and fallen and sought to remove the occasion for wars. Indeed, along with their rejection of war, the Historic Peace churches—as Mennonites, Quakers, and Brethren have been called since 1935—are best known for their extensive programs of relief, reconstruction, and reconciliation. Far beyond what their small numerical size might indicate, they have mounted highly significant efforts to assist the victims of war and oppression as well as of natural catastrophes. Quaker relief to the people of the Soviet Union, Brethren help to the Armenians, and Mennonite assistance in postwar Vietnam are examples of such outreach.

In addition, this peace testimony has taken other forms of expression. Pioneering efforts in work camps, international exchange, and far-flung voluntary services programs have given concrete, practical assistance across the boundaries of race, nation, and class. The first department of peace studies in the U.S. began in 1948 at Manchester College, a Brethren related school. Civil disobedience and other forms of nonviolent resistance to war have likewise been fostered by peace church members.

But as we bring this brief survey up to the present time, there is a striking new development spreading among the churches. Peacemaking, even in its radical pacifist expression, has come to be seen more and more as central to the Christian calling. This is due in part to the breakdown of the whole idea of Christian civilization. In an era of totalitarianism, global war, genocide, and possible nuclear annihilation, Christian witness is often seen as a distinct minority position. The radical reformation understanding of the church as a disciplined community within the wider society is gaining acceptance as both biblically rooted and urgently appropriate to the type of discipleship needed in such a world as ours. This is seen nowhere more clearly than with regards to the runaway development of weapons technology. It is like a Frankenstein monster that has taken over the direction of the nation state in the last half of the twentieth century with a momentum and justification of its own. A permanent arms race, global arms sales, nuclear weapons of mass destruction pose extreme threats to the very future of our planet.

The traditional just war theory seems less and less plausible in the face of such awesome destructiveness. As a result, Christians from a variety of traditions, even in the theocratic state churches, are taking up a more radical peacemaking stance. The peace pastoral of the Roman Catholic bishops is only one indication of what has happened in the Catholic church, especially since the remarkable papacy of John XXIII. Religious orders and communities, such as Catholic Worker Houses and other groups, are involved not only in peace education, but in nonviolent direct action and various forms of civil disobedience.

The Presbyterians have established peace as their denominational priority and have developed a far-reaching peace strategy from the local to the national level. The United Church of Christ is seriously grappling with what it means to be a "peace church" as is the Disciples of Christ which, incidentally, is recovering its early tradition that is closely akin to that of the Historic Peace Churches. Among the Baptists, especially the American Baptist Convention but also a vigorous number of

Southern Baptists, peacemaking in the life of believers is growing in a widening circle. The same is true for a remarkable number of evangelicals, as well as Episcopalians, Lutherans, United Methodists, Reformed and Unitarian-Universalists. Among the black denominations, the strong involvement in civil rights has begun to be broadened to include peacemaking as well. In short, across a broad spectrum of the religious community, peacemaking has moved in recent years to the center of the church's witness in society.

A similar development can be seen in other places of the world as well. Throughout Europe the churches have been at the forefront of a growing peace movement. Dutch Christians for example are committed to a world free of nuclear weapons, "beginning with the Netherlands." East German pacifists witness against militarism while West German Christians oppose the deployment of Cruise and Pershing missiles. The Russian Orthodox Church convened a world assembly on peace and fosters a growing relationship with European and North American Christians to rid the world of nuclear weapons "East and West." The World Council of Churches and the Vatican are becoming more forceful in their peace advocacy.

If peace seems at last to have moved front and center in the church's life and witness, many are asking if there is anything remaining that is distinctive about the peace churches and their message? First, the fact that peace has moved toward the center of the wider church's witness makes it imperative that the Historic Peace Churches find ways of sharing their biblical understanding, their historical experience and the avenues of witness and service they have developed. Many Christians newly committed to peacemaking, are still accustomed to the church playing a dominant role in society, aligned with the powers that be; the experience of the Historic Peace churches as a faithful, prophetic minority provide a needed alternative model. The rejection of war is not a peculiar and optional ethical issue but rather is the clearest indication of the church's calling to be a community free from the domination and manipulation of the state and living the life of radical discipleship. Such radical discipleship, if we are to believe the New Testament, embraces those on the other side of the dividing walls of hostility in our world, even including the enemy.

At this point, it seems to me, the message of the Historic Peace Churches should be sharp and unambiguous. While the growing peace consciousness is highly significant the needed shift in society has yet to occur. Many Christian peacemakers in our time are still deeply aligned with the nation state and accept weapons of mass destruction. As significant as the Catholic Bishops Peace Pastoral is, it still finds a place for nuclear weapons and their deterrent role. As encouraging as ecumenical outreach to the USSR is, many such Christians still say, "We don't need the MX and the Trident submarine we have already far more weapons than is necessary to wipe out the Soviet Union." Overkill is rejected; obliteration is not. Many Christians consider themselves to be nuclear pacifists but still justify other weapons of mass destruction. And many, many advocate a nuclear weapons freeze but are unwilling to consider, much less advocate, disarmament except under the most cautious, bilateral circumstances.

So while there is much to rejoice at in the widespread peace movement in the churches today, the Historic Peace Churches should be on the cutting edge of this movement, seeking to live out the implications of the way of the nonviolent cross. This is a way that calls Christians to love the enemy, to aid the oppressed, to enter the struggle for justice and liberation, and to partake of the Beloved community that knows no boundary.

Richard Daggett Deats
Fellowship of Reconciliation

Preface

This book was conceived as a revision of *Brethren and Paci fism*, published by Brethren Press in 1970. Like so many of our endeavors, however, its final shape is much different from its original plan. Like old sermons retrieved from a musty barrel, it was not merely the illustrations that were dated. The content and basic organization needed to be re-formed. The context had also changed. The readers were different. The first book was written for Church of the Brethren members and their youth who were struggling with the meaning of the peace witness in the midst of the Vietnam tragedy. This book offers biblical perspectives of the peace churches to Christians of other traditions, who are increasingly involved in the things that make for peace.

New Brethren readers, of course, will want to read the whole thing. Those who have read the previous book can easily skip over chapter two. Others may prefer to skip case study scenarios of the Brethren and begin with chapter three, an analysis of the variety of interpretations of the peace church heritage. Though the book lacks extensive prooftexting and quotations from scripture, there remains a conscious intention to apply basic biblical themes to critical issues facing peacemakers. Following a presentation of biblical motifs, subsequent chapters address the nuclear crisis, liberation movements, and our stance toward the state in the terms of biblical faith, hope and love. Finally, shalom lifestyles are presented in areas of spirituality, families, evangelism, conflict resolution, questions related to war taxes, and basic views of violence in personal relationships. The popular "What If?" chapter of the previous book has been revised, expanded and included here as an Epilogue. The appendices contain basic documents of the historic peace churches.

As I wrote and meditated, I was often gripped by a sense of urgency. Biblical and contemporary imperatives for peacemaking converged. I was also filled with thanksgiving as I discerned the growing number of saints and signs of the peaceable kingdom. Still I remain humbled by the magnitude of the crisis, the prevalence of violence, and the worship of gods of wars. I am led to confess anew that our salvation will only come as God's power is manifest through our weaknesses. I owe special thanks to Dale Aukerman and Richard Gardner whose reactions to the previous book contributed greatly to the format of this one. It has been a privilege to work with James Lehman, who carefully reviewed the final manuscript, and David Eller, a book editor who is deeply committed to the things that make for peace.

Dale W. Brown
Lombard, Illinois

1

A Peace Church and the Peace Churches

A Roman Catholic friend of mine frequently reminds me that he too is a member of a peace church. Since Pope John XXIII and Vatican II, I have often felt closer to Catholic pacifists than to those in my own tradition. I know of one community in which Catholic peace activists regularly participate in the Church of the Brethren Love Feast. During the last decade I have sometimes mused that communities supporting periodicals such as *Sojourners* and *Radix* are more authentic carriers of the peace church tradition than many of us who identify ourselves as direct descendants. The Church of the Brethren is often defined theologically as a synthesis of Anabaptism with the Pietist reformation. Yet, what more beautiful expression of the same can be found than in the kingdom theology of Eberhard Arnold, founder of the twentieth century Hutterian Society of Brothers.

More recently I have been gratified that many so-called mainline denominations are threatening to become peace churches. The Christian Church (Disciples of Christ) has debated whether they want to be known officially as a peace church. In dealing with a similar motion by a youth delegate, the United Church of Christ presently prefers to be called a "just peace church" instead of just another peace church. The Presbyterians have spent some million dollars for peace education and activity. Methodists are experiencing a revival of their long-held deep concerns for peace. Vocal peace minorities are emerging among the Lutherans, Baptists, Episcopalians, Jews, and others. Realistically, the major denominations are far from having a strong unified peace position. Still they are moving toward it, not away from it.

To this role call, one would need to add Christian forerunners: the large majority in the church in the first three centuries, the Franciscans within and the "heretical" Waldensians outside the Western Church, the Moravians, denominations emerging from the holiness and Finney movements such as the Wesleyan Methodists, and many pockets of biblical pacifists among the Pentecostals in the first part of this century.

In 1935 the term "Historic Peace Churches" was coined to designate the collective pacifist convictions of the Mennonites, Friends, and Brethren. "Mennonite" here means primarily those Mennonite groups that make up the Mennonite Central Committee, including the Brethren in Christ. Though portions of this book will focus on the Church of the Brethren peace witness, references to the peace church tradition will generally encompass the above three traditions.

Encountering such growing commitment to peacemaking by many varieties of Christians has moved me to struggle anew with my peace church identity. In reading Richards Deat's complimentary foreword to this book, I vacillated between feeling pride and squirming in my chair as his description of our heritage at its best became a judgment on our present life. Do these peace churches continue as living witnesses to the gospel of peace? What do the Brethren and the peace church tradition have to offer and say to others? In a book dedicated to this heritage, the best way to begin is with confession.

Confessions of Failure and of Faith

The Church of the Brethren—a peace church! For many, such a statement seems hypocritical. In some communities pacifist Brethren feel more kinship with peacemakers of other traditions than with members of their own congregations. Some Brethren youth, who attempt to embody their peace heritage, have been forced to find inspiration, songs, leadership, and models of action outside their community of faith. Sizable portions of Brethren hold the "peace through strength" philosophy and support the call for armaments of the so-called "moral majority."

Nevertheless, the weight of tradition stands solidly behind the peace witness. Never has the consensus of a major Brethren meeting or conference deviated from a strong pacifist statement.

The leadership is unified on this issue as on few others. It has been estimated that from ninety to ninety-six percent of Brethren pastors subscribe to the church's peace position. This deep peace concern is the motivating force behind the extensive service ministries of the Church of the Brethren as well as its recent cooperation with the other two peace churches in the New Call to Peacemaking.

A common way to point to the growing acculturation of the Brethren has been to cite statistics showing how eighteen-year-old members have responded to conscription. Various surveys have estimated the percentage of those drafted choosing the armed forces from eighty to ninety percent during world War II to some sixty percent in the Vietnam era. Though there is need for more research, such evidence points to a change from an earlier time when promises to refuse to prepare for or participate in war were made at the time of baptism.

As is usually the case, there is another way to interpret the statistics! It may not be wise for any tradition to determine the degree of faithfulness by what eighteen-year-old members do or believe. But even if we do, ten to forty percent of two hundred thousand Brethren means from twenty to eighty thousand peacemakers. What a potential movement! Instead of decrying the present state let us commit ourselves to shoe these thousands of feet with the "equipment of the gospel of peace" (Eph. 6:15).

Still we must confess that we have often defined peace as avoiding trouble instead of overcoming evil with good. We have been content to be just peace churches instead of rooting our witness in biblical justice. Between wars we have often neglected the things that make for peace only to cry peace, peace when our own youth are threatened with the draft. In our desire to be respectable we have been too timid.

Nevertheless, we reaffirm the relevance of the witness we have been given not only against the nuclear threat but against conventional wars and the pervading cultural infatuation with violence. For us the peace testimony has not been an appendage to our faith, but an organic outgrowth. We rejoice in the current widespread call to peacemaking by brothers and sisters in the larger body of Christ. However, we want to be true to our historic calling and make sure the current interest is rooted deep in the nourishing soil of our Judeo-Christian faith.

Yet those of us who are most zealous in espousing our peace heritage confess that we sometimes make an idol out of peace instead of proclaiming the peace of God. We worship our schemes for peace instead of participating in God's peaceable kingdom.

Nevertheless, we are not ashamed to be identified with pacifism, which comes from two Latin roots, *pax* (peace) and *facere* (to make). Pacifism, which literally means peacemaking, remains a sound biblical word in spite of perversions by its adherents and negative interpretations by opponents. We recognize the scandalous nature of the peace witness as the Apostle Paul saw the scandal and foolishness of the way of powerless love. Furthermore, pacifists are not alone in idolizing their ideas of right and wrong, for it takes a great amount of eating from the tree of the knowledge of good and evil to know with certainty what is right and wrong to the degree that one may exterminate another human life.

The Ecumenical Context

When I invited a professor to share his faith heritage with one of my classes, he replied: "It should be the other way around, for you belong to an historic peace tradition which is the most relevant in our present context." His statement represents a shifting mood. As one who has been invited to speak about my pacifist convictions to a variety of audiences, I sense a change in attitude since the national debate over Vietnam. Then I frequently served as a pacifist exhibit to represent a minority view beside a just war theorist and Christian advocate for the war. Even many who were against that war were not about to buy my stance. Instead they complimented themselves and America for the kind of tolerance that allowed a peculiar sectarian like me to espouse way-out views. Now, instead of being asked to satisfy curiosity about pacifists, I am invited to share the biblical and theological bases of peacemaking to persons genuinely seeking to know more about the things that make for peace.

One cannot help but be gratified by this. Longtime peace advocates are inspired by the present peace movement's grass-roots organizations, professional groups, and ardent worldwide demonstrations. From past experience, however, we know how quickly such popular sentiment can dissipate into illusory peace gestures or evaporate in heated patriotic fervor.

A talk-back radio show played on into the wee hours of the morning. Callers discussed the morality of war from many perspectives. I was confined to my automobile and could not respond. The tragedy was that not one caller suggested that the Christian gospel might bear some relevance to the issue. Where was the witness of the peace churches?

M. R. Zigler, long time Brethren representative to the World Council of Churches and peace veteran, offered an example of opportunities for such a witness. He testified that on numerous occasions outstanding church leaders tapped him to make a speech they wished to have made but preferred not to risk at that particular time. Many peace church delegates can testify with Zigler that no minor part of the power of the witness is the fact that one does not speak as an individual but on behalf of a tradition and a people.

Some Brethren would prefer to lose their denominational identity and become a part of a growing pacifist minority in the church universal. Most, however, like the majority of Christians, find a rationale or rationalization to continue as a separate denomination. Look at the perceptive analysis of Otto Piper, who served as a biblical theologian for many years at Princeton Theological seminary. He wrote:

> We have no doubt, however, that notwithstanding serious self-scrutiny there will be instances in which a denomination must reach the conclusion that the specific contribution it makes to the life of the Protestant church is sufficiently important to warrant its continued existence. The facile manner in which the termination of the Protestant denominations is advocated

by some ecclesiastical leaders is a symptom of the modern belief in mammoth organizations rather than of a spiritual zeal for church unity. One criterion by which the right of existence of denominations is to be measured is the role they have played in holy history. Whenever it can be stated that the history of Protestantism would have been essentially different had it not been for the contribution made by a specific denomination, one is entitled to see their role as the work of the risen Lord. Such a denomination has a spiritual and historical right to independent existence and only two reasons could oblige it to terminate that existence: if that denomination repentantly realizes that it has irretrievably lost its original spiritual momentum and thus is no longer capable of making its specific contribution, or if it is obvious that a specific gift it has to impart has so completely become the common property of the whole Protestant church that no special denominational agency for its propagation is required.

Yet we have to reckon *a priori* with the likelihood that a number of denominations will be *bona fide* entitled to continue their work because they bring out an aspect of the Christian faith which no other denomination represents, the complete absence of which would result in a serious impoverishment of Protestantism. Of course, such evaluation would apply to the present situation only and would not entail the necessity of a denomination's permanent existence. But in the light of contemporary experience one can safely state, for instance, that without the peace witness of Quakers, Mennonites, and Brethren, Protestantism would lack one of the essential marks of the gospel message. In turn, however, although the outcome of such self-examination may justify the continued existence of a denomination, it can never mean a continuation of what it was like prior to such scrutiny.[1]

A careful reading of Piper's analysis will not comfort those who argue against church merger in order to maintain the peace witness as we now have it. Christians both inside and outside of the peace churches need to be open to the scrutiny Piper calls for and the resulting openness to change.

John Howard Yoder, Mennonite scholar, in a keynote address to a meeting of the historic peace churches, dealt with this same issue. For him the issue of war and killing is more basic to the heart of the biblical message than many other ethical and doctrinal concerns. In matters of faith and practice on which Christians differ, it is difficult to find another like killing in warfare where Christians sanction a position which we believe is immoral. Yoder concludes:

> What other heresy or what other sin is being institutionalized as is preparation for war? What other heresy or sin is destroying the church, dividing the church, destroying men with such a claim to be rightous? The fact is that there is none is not a matter of taste or of historical accidents which somehow regrettably came to pass. It is one of official denominational positions, and it must provide some kind of justification for the distinctive degree of common concern among those who are a very small minority on this issue.[2]

Eileen Egan, an editor of *The Catholic Worker*, speaks more positively of the contribution of the peace churches than those of us inside can imagine we deserve. Attending the first New Call to Peacemaking conference of the peace churches in 1978, she enthusiastically shared with me her historical perspective. Speaking out of a tradition which traces its roots to the apostle Peter, she affirmed that Roman Catholics were pacifists for the first three centuries. Then Constantine and Augustine borrowed the just war theory from the pagans in order to allow lay Christians to become soldiers. But, she added, the pacifist witness was retained by nearly all the clergy and religious orders for over a millenium. At the time of the reformation the historic peace churches emerged to reclaim this wonderful testimony for all Christians. And now, she exulted, you are giving back to us the witness we had in the beginning.

Whether within their own circles or with other Christians, peace church members are abandoning their isolationist stance to participate in ecumenical structures and dialogue. They have been in continuing consultation with the World Council of Churches on questions of violence, nonviolence and the struggle for social justice. They have insisted that a sign and witness to unity would be for Christians to love one another. When M. R.

Zigler found himself in the midst of debates concerning creeds, communion, ministry, and baptism, he often rose to his feet and proposed that Lutherans pledge to refuse to kill other Lutherans, Anglicans other Anglicans, etc. His motions were not taken seriously because he was suspected of a pacifist ploy. In our world, however, what more powerful testimony to the unity of the church could there be than a serious pledge by Christians to refuse to kill other Christians.

However, the New Testament word for ecumenical does not just refer to the internal life and unity within the Christian community. *Oikoumene* denotes the world to which the church is called and sent. It is the space in which the church moves, the sphere of God's action. *Oikoumene* stands for the communion of the church with the enemy, with the portion of humanity which, in utter selfishness, stands opposed to the gospel.

Here the testimony of the peace tradition about loving enemies becomes relevant. We are at one with other Christians in seeking to discern what Christ means for us today. We struggle with similar issues—abortion, sexuality, domestic violence, alleged or real threats to the family structure, the nuclear threat, theologies of liberation, and polarization over economic and political trends.

Thus this book will be ecumenical in the broadest sense of the word. The early chapters will deal with the history of a peace church struggling to respond to the demands of powers and principalities, with the varieties of stances found within the biblical peace tradition, and with some key biblical motifs which have shaped the peace witness. Subsequent chapters will deal with manifestations of structural violence, liberation theologies, the nuclear threat and the arms race, political structures and styles of resistance, and the integration of personal and social *shalom* (salvation, wholeness, peace, justice).

2

The Pacifist Heritage of the Brethren

Before his small cadre became the Sojourner's community, Jim Wallis inquired about the peace church heritage. He stated honestly that his community had no interest in joining the Church of the Brethren. They were, however, most attracted to our history. They were intrigued by simple evangelical believers with strong peace and justice concerns.

The first eight Brethren baptized in the Eder river near Schwarzenau were not, by that act, breaking away from the State churches of the German territories. Rather, they were already separatists and had been refugees for a period. Their study of the Scriptures had convinced them they should form a church community. How else could they faithfully follow the method of settling disputes set forth in Matthew 18:15-19. From the beginning the Brethren were committed to the ministry of reconciliation, and this text came to be read at the time of baptism. They were influenced by the love theology of the Pietists. They were disgusted by the devastating religious wars, and polemical apologetics of the established churches. But they rejected Pietism's individualism and gathered a church, thus identifying consciously with the nonresistant Anabaptist wing of the older Reformation. In this milieu the peace pilgrimage of the people called Brethren began.

Anabaptism

The word Anabaptist, which literally means "to rebaptize," points to the specific crime for which the former Zwinglians who became the Mennonites were charged when the first congregation came into being in Switzerland in 1525. But the name is used in a much broader sense to designate those beliefs and movements which have come to be known as the radical or left wing of the Protestant Reformation.[1] The fact that the first Brethren in Europe were called "New Baptists" reveals their similarity with the Mennonites and others who came from the Anabaptist wing of the sixteenth-century Reformation.[2] The Brethren affirmed such central Anabaptist themes as: The essence of Christianity is radical discipleship; the nature of the church is voluntary brotherhood; and the life-style of Christians is love and sharing.

The "New German Baptists" followed the old Baptists in their nonresistance stance. Some of the sixteenth-century radicals had attempted to bring in the kingdom by the use of the sword. A group established an armed fortress at Munster, Germany, in 1534. Thomas Muntzer led the peasants in a war against their princes in 1525. However, the main groups of Anabaptists and their Amish and Mennonite descendants adopted a position of nonresistance, renouncing the use of the sword in all its forms.

Nonresistance was a major item in the Schleitheim Confession of Faith, prepared at a conference of Anabaptist Swiss Brethren in 1527. The confession also stated that a Christian could not be a magistrate, responsible for either judging or executing sentences in the disputes of the world. The reasons given were Christ's refusal to pass judgment in the case of the inheritance and his rejection of the role of a political king. This view supported the early Anabaptist and Brethren prejudice against participation in power structures. The use of the sword for punishing the wicked and protecting the good might be necessary outside the perfection of Christ, but for members of the obedient brotherhood, such action was not permissible.

Yet love required more than refusal to participate in the major structures of society. It called for the creation of a new society where peace and brotherhood would reign. State churches called upon the magistrate to punish by death or exile persons who were guilty of doctrinal or ecclesiastical deviation. But the voluntary brotherhood of the church was not to use such means. Instead, the Anabaptist community instituted the ban, based on Matthew 18. The errant member was excluded from communion (the smaller ban) or excluded from membership (the greater ban). The ban as a form of discipline may seem harsh today, but in the sixteenth century it was an extremely humane and liberal method as is suggested in the following statement from the Schleitheim Confession: "In the perfection of Christ, however, only the ban is used for a warning and for the excommunication of the one who has sinned, without putting to death—simply the warning and the command to sin no more.[3]"

Because of their beliefs and their break with the established churches, the early Anabaptists were tortured, drowned, hanged, burned at the stake, imprisoned, and exiled. Despite such severe and systematic persecution, Anabaptism was threatening to become a mass religious movement. It is natural that Anabaptists developed a theology of martyrdom, since every meeting was regarded as a possible last farewell to the persons in their fellowship. Their baptism could be a literal baptism unto death. Their imitation of Christ could lead to drinking his cup of suffering and taking up the cross. For them discipleship meant suffering in the spirit of the cross. Their pacifism was derived, in part, from their conviction that they could not bear to inflict on others the brutal violence which they were forced to endure.

The Brethren, who came later and were never persecuted as severely as their sixteenth- and seventeenth-century forerunners, did not develop a theology of suffering to the same degree. But the Schwarzenau Brethren in 1708 identified with the Anabaptist way. Alexander Mack, one of the original eight, responded to an inquiry about the former Anabaptists in question 40 of his *Basic Questions*. Speaking of the Lutherans, Calvinists, and Catholics, he wrote: "What is still more horrible, they go publicly to war, and slaughter one another by the thousands." But of the older Baptists, he affirmed: "No Baptist will be found in war."[4]

The Pietist Environment

In addition to this conscious identification with the older Anabaptist movement, the early Brethren were influenced by the Pietist Reformation in the Lutheran and Reformed churches in the last decades of the seventeenth century and in early years of the eighteenth century. Philipp Jakob Spener launched this reform movement within the Lutheran church in Germany in 1675 with the publication of his book *Pious Desires*. He stressed greater lay participation, Bible study groups, and true regeneration in reaction to the rigid orthodoxy, religious fighting, and moral decadence following the terrible Thirty Years' War. The Pietists insisted that the reformation of doctrine which had come with Luther must be carried through to a reformation of life.

Some of the Pietist themes were similar to Anabaptism. This is demonstrated by the fact that Pietism flourished in the areas which had been the strongholds of the sixteenth-century radicals. August Hermann Francke also gave the Pietist movement shape through his educational, charitable, and missionary activities and through the many institutions he founded at the University of Halle in Germany.[5]

Some Pietists despaired of ever reforming the church from within. They became separatists with more radical ideas. Contrary to Spener and Francke, who were churchly Pietists, they have been called radical Pietists. Most of the early Brethren in Europe had at first identified with the radicals. In forming a new brotherhood, they brought with them radical Pietist ideas such as non-creedalism, the universal restoration of all souls, the sharing of goods, an emphasis on the powerful working of the Holy Spirit and a deep devotion to Jesus as Lord and Savior. Because many of the radical Pietists were also pacifists, it is important to recognize that their teachings may have influenced the early Brethren.

Pacifism Among the Radical Pietists. Jacob Boehme (1575-1624) has been regarded as an ideological father of radical Pietism. For Boehme the institutional church was Babel. In no way should religion be controlled by the state. Christians should not participate in the wars of Babel. Boehme divided the history of the world into six previous ages. He felt that the seventh age of peace and unity was near and that Christians should begin to live in the reality of this expectation. Hochman von Hochenau, saintly friend and associate of Alexander Mack, interpreted the call of Christ to mean the refusal of military service if conscripted.

Gottfried Arnold (1666-1714), the church historian read by Mack and probably other Brethren, was the first to write favorably of the nonresistant Anabaptists. His pacifism was a part of a longing to find in the primitive church of the first three centuries contemporary models of Christian life. For him, the fall had come with the union of church and state under Constantine at the beginning of the fourth century. A special tragedy befell this gentle preacher late in his ministry; Prussian recruiting officers rushed into his church and seized all the young men present, drafting them on the spot and taking them away for military duty.

Brethren historians have debated and disagreed over the degree of Pietist versus Anabaptist influence. Whatever the answer, it is probably true that Brethren convictions have been strongest when both strands have been present in equal measure. For example, the peace position was strengthened by the Anabaptists' desire to restore the model and beliefs of the early church and by the Pietists' knowledge of the life of the early Christians. At the same time there were basic differences that account for tensions which have remained to the present. Whereas the Anabaptists modeled a revitalized fellowship but expected little change in unredeemed society, the Pietists hoped for better times for both church and state. Though Pietists may have held to a more pessimistic view of human nature, their times led them to greater optimism about what God might be able to do through the redemption of persons and the world.

The Historical Context. The peace position of the early Brethren cannot be understood fully apart from an understanding of the political, social, and economic conditions of that time. The memory of the terrible Thirty Years' War (1618-1648) was vivid. This war, in part a religious war of Protestants against Catholics, was one of the worst in history. The psychological impact on its survivors and their posterity was immense. Some estimates have the population decreasing by three quarters and show the loss of livestock and wealth to be even greater. Anarchy was common in much of Germany. There were many areas of Germany which were practically depopulated.

The war was morally destructive, economically disastrous, and socially degrading. Unfortunately, the end of this war did not bring peace to the Germanies. The remainder of the seventeenth century was a turbulent and unsettled time. The peasants grew weary of armies' plundering their fields, as in 1688 when the armies of Louis XIV swept over the Palatinate.

Spener and Francke, early Pietists who remained with the church to attempt a reformation from within, opposed the immorality of the church leadership and the bitter doctrinal disputes. They deplored the street fighting and the vulgarity of university students. They hated the practice of selling subjects as troops to foreign nations and the arbitrary methods of military conscription used by German sovereigns.

Princes dominated church affairs and frequently persecuted dissenters. The Treaty of Westphalia (1648), which ended the war specified that the ruler determine the religion, choosing either the Reformed, the Lutheran, or the Catholic faith. All subjects had to belong to the church of their ruler or migrate to a territory with one of the other two options.

Because of the lack of population and the depressing economic conditions, there were a few rulers who practiced religious tolerance in order to attract settlers. Such was the case in Wittgenstein and the village of Schwarzenau, the birthplace of the Brethren. In times of famine, plagues, plunder, persecution, and violence, there often emerges among sensitive people a mood of revulsion against war. A peace movement comes into being which proclaims a new theology of hope. This, was no doubt, one reason why the Church of the Brethren, coming out of such a historical period, adopted a position rejecting war and stressing reconciling love.

The Brethren in Europe

The story of the tall Brethren elder, John Naas, illustrates the position of the founders in Germany. Recruiting officers cap-

tured and tortured Naas, then dragged him before the king of
Prussia. "Tell me, why will you not enlist with me?" inquired
the king. "Because," said Naas, "I have already, long ago,
enlisted into one of the noblest and best of enrollments, and I
would not, and indeed could not, become a traitor to Him."
"Why, to whom, then? Who is your captain?" asked the aston-
ished king. "My captain," replied Naas, "is the great Prince
Immanuel, our Lord Jesus Christ. I have espoused his cause and
therefore cannot, and will not, forsake him." "Neither will I
then that you should," answered the king, who presented him
with a handsome gold coin as a reward for his faithfulness to his
Lord.

The historical accuracy of this story is somewhat suspect, as
we know of it only through an article by A. H. Cassel in *The
Brethren Family Almanac* (1871, p. 24), but its teaching is very
much in the Anabaptist vein. Obedience to Jesus comes prior to
any other consideration. In this story the name of John Naas may
have been attached to an earlier account of a member in Europe.
A document to support this is found in a collection by a Quaker
historian of the province of Pennsylvania from 1751 to 1775, an
account which antedated Cassel's story by over a hundred years:

> During these persecutions the king of Prussia had granted a
> general liberty of conscience, but his press-gangs, or soldiers
> on recruiting parties, vexed them sorely several times. One
> John Fisher from Hall, who had been baptized, they would
> force against his conscience to list in the king's service, and
> tormented him terribly for ten days together, different ways,
> because he would not comply with their wills, they tied his
> hands and feet together and by them hung him up, thrusting
> and beating him with sticks and pricking his body with pins to
> such a degree that his shirt became stiff with blood, and when
> he was quite faint and could stand no longer on his legs, they
> put him near a deep water and he tumbling into it, they pulled
> him out again by his legs, but at last when they had tired
> themselves with tormenting of him, and he still refusing to
> swear to the colours and take arms, they threw him into a
> hole, where the prince of Dessan happening himself to come
> by, and seeing him in such a sad condition told them to let him
> go, for he had suffered his torment.[6]

Whatever the historicity of the details of these stories, their telling shows that the pacifist tradition was passed from early to subsequent generations.

Brethren in the American Colonies

In Germantown, Pennsylvania both Mennonites and Brethren enjoyed complete religious freedom and were not subject to any form of military conscription under Quaker rule. Several early histories of the Pennsylvania sects stress the fact that pacifism was one of the main beliefs of the Brethren. The statement by Samuel Smith, the Quaker historian, is typical: "They hold it not becoming a follower of Jesus Christ to bear arms or fight since their true Master has forbidden his disciples to resist evil . . ."[7]

The Brethren were strengthened in their pacifism, no doubt, by their Mennonite neighbors and Quaker rulers. Both the Mennonites and the Brethren voted to keep the Quakers in power. Their beliefs were nurtured by the Radical Pietist printer, the elder Christopher Sauer, who was uncompromising in his pacifism. In various pamphlets, Sauer praised the nonresistant disciples of Christ, supported the peaceful policies of William Penn and his successors against the attacks of men like Benjamin Franklin, and urged the German-speaking people to support the beneficent government. A true follower of Christ, he asserted, may not kill even a French murderer who is attacking him. He can only trust in God's protection. Participation in war, therefore, is contrary to the gospel. Sauer spoke of soldiers as military slaves.

Though we do not have an abundance of pacifist literature from the colonial Brethren, the following poem from the writings of Michael Frantz, a Swiss immigrant who was baptized by Peter Becker in 1734, may be an early variation of a contemporary slogan, "Suppose they gave a war and nobody came."

> When men of war do violence to none,
> Then will war soon cease;
> You should not do wrong to anyone,

So that you may rest from war.
But now shalt Christ's community
Be quite defenseless against the outward sword;
It has here no worldly right,
To fight for such is much too wicked.
One should not take up the sword,
And, even if one has to face trial,
One must be more obedient to God
Than to the rest of mankind together.
Defenseless, free of the world and sinless,
Of a humble heart and not at all puffed up,
This is how God would have his community,
Kept pure from Babel's stain and spots.[8]

Early Brethren communities faced their first real trials during the French and Indian War and the Indian massacres in the last decades of the eighteenth century. U. J. Jones, historian of the Pennsylvania Commonwealth, wrote in detail of the massacre of Brethren by the Indians at Morrison's Cove, which occurred between 1777 and 1780. He described them as strict nonresistants who "not only refused to take up arms to repel the savage marauders and prevent the inhuman slaughter of women and children, but they refused in the most positive manner to pay a dollar to support those who were willing to take up arms to defend their homes and their firesides, until wrung from them by the stern mandates of the law, from which there was no appeal."[9]

Brethren had, however, responded to Sauer's appeal through his columns to comply with the requisition in 1758 of wagons and horses from German farms. But in reference to their own direct participation, the author gives the following graphic account of the puzzling Dunkards:

On their first expedition they would have few scalps to grace their belts, had the Dunkards taken the advice of more sagacious people, and fled, too; this however, they would not do. They would follow but half of Cromwell's advice; they were willing to put their "trust in God," but they would not "keep their powder dry." In short, it was a compound they did not use at all.

> The savages (Indians) swept down through the Cove with all
> the ferocity with which a pack of wolves would descend
> from the mountain upon a flock of sheep. Some few of the
> Dunkards, who evidently had a latent spark of love of life,
> hid themselves away; but by far the most of them stood by
> and witnessed the butchery of wives and children, merely
> saying, "Gottes Willes sei gethan." How many Dunkard
> scalps they carried to Detroit cannot now be, and probably
> never has been clearly ascertained—not less than thirty,
> according to the best authority.[10]

Again, this story points to the Dunkards' acceptance of the
nonresistance stance of Anabaptism. They were obedient to
Christ's command to "resist not evil."

Brethren and the American Revolution

The American Revolution brought troubled times for all of
the peace groups in the colonies. They were accused of Toryism,
loyalty to the king of England, because, as good citizens, they
obeyed the crown. Although the Continental Congress and the
Pennsylvania assembly did not require military service from religious conscientious objectors, the feelings of the "associators,"
the active supporters of the revolution, became more belligerent
toward the peace groups. In some instances mob violence broke
out against Mennonites in parts of Lancaster County. In this
atmosphere of growing hostility, Mennonite and Brethren elders
joined together to present a petition to the newly elected provin-
cial assembly. The English translation which was handed to the
assembly on November 7, 1775, began by thanking God and the
assembly for granting liberty of conscience as had William Penn
to those who "are persuaded in their conscience to love their
enemies, and not to resist evil . . ."

The petition suggested, perhaps for the first time in Brethren history, a basis for an alternative service stand:

> The advice to those who do not find Freedom of conscience to
> take up arms, that they ought to be helpful to those who are in
> need and distressed circumstances, we receive with cheerful-
> ness towards all men of what station they may be—it being our

principle to feed the Hungry and give the Thirsty Drink,—we
have dedicated ourselves to serve all men in everything that
can be helpful to the preservation of Men's Lives, but we find
no Freedom in giving, or doing, or assisting in any thing by
which Men's Lives are destroyed or hurt.[11]

The petition concluded with the assertion that they would be
willing to pay taxes to Caesar and to be subject to the higher
powers in all things lawful. There was likewise an Anabaptist
recognition of the legitimate authority of the state in asserting
that the ruler "beareth the sword not in vain, for he is the minister of God, a Revenger to execute wrath upon him that doeth
evil."[12]

In spite of this petition, the opposition grew against nonas-
sociators who refused to participate in the rebellion against
England. The assembly required all males refusing to bear arms
to contribute an amount of money equivalent to the time others
gave in acquiring military discipline. A few months later it
decreed that all weapons should be collected from nonparticip-
ants. Then, in the spirit of intense patriotism, the assembly
required an oath of allegiance in an act passed June 13, 1777.
Each male above the age of fifteen was to subscribe to an oath
renouncing allegiance to George the Third, king of Great Brit-
ain, and declaring faithful allegiance to the Commonwealth of
Pennsylvania as a free and independent state. The oath included
a promise to report all traitorous conspiracies to a justice of
peace.

How did the Brethren respond to these pressures? It may be
a shocking scandal to many to learn that the first recorded decision of an annual meeting forbade Brethren to take an oath of
allegiance to the new country. The 1778 annual meeting at Pipe
Creek, Maryland, requested the Brethren who had taken the
attest (or oath) to recall it before a justice, give up their certifi-
cate, and apologize in their churches. Refusal to do so would
mean that the brother would be deprived of the kiss of fellowship
and the breaking of bread.

It was for his refusal to take the oath of allegiance to the
States that Elder Christopher Sauer Jr. saw his press and prop-

erty, estimated at one hundred fifty thousand dollars, confiscated and destroyed. He himself was arrested, suffered humilating treatment at the hands of the Revolutionary army, and died a poor man among the Brethren. The fact that his two sons, who did not join the church, sided openly with the British added to the suspicions that he had Tory leanings. His name appears in the Pennsylvania archives under the heading, "Persons Gone With Ye Enemy."

The 1780 big meeting at Conestoga forbade members to pay "substitute money" which was used by some who refused military service to hire someone else to go in their place. Paying such a substitute was considered wrong since it did not differ morally from direct participation.[13] In the following year, however, it was reported that the decision had been disregarded here and there. The yearly meeting in 1781 dealt more completely with this issue and several others related to the war. The meeting repeated its instruction to "take no part in war or bloodshedding, which might take place if we would pay for hiring men voluntarily." The new government had been threatening the Brethren with heavy fines in order to collect such money. The meeting urged the Brethren not to be afraid to stand for their principles. And to make this possible, it was agreed that heavy fines imposed on Brethren who refused to cooperate would be the collective responsibility of the congregations. But the decision stopped short of complete resistance. "In case a brother or his son should be drafted, that he or his son should go to war, and he could buy himself or his son from it, such would not be deemed so sinful, yet it should not be given voluntarily, without compulsion."[14]

Brethren today who refuse war taxes only to have them taken involuntarily from their bank accounts or payroll checks are more in the tradition of these early Brethren than they perhaps realize. The same Annual Meeting (1781) dealt also with the matter of a special tax to support the war. The Conference was permissive, recognizing the differences which evidently existed among the Brethren on this point: "In order to avoid offense, we might follow the example of Christ (Matt. 17:24-27), yet if one does not see it so, and thinks, perhaps, he for his conscience' sake could not pay it, but bear with others who pay, in patience, we would willingly leave it over, inasmuch we deem the overruling of the conscience as wrong."[15]

The peace people were misunderstood because each side thought they supported the other side. The Brethren were consistent in their refusal to bear arms. They were not as consistent in refusing to pay for substitutes to take their place. For the most part they refused the original request but paid subsequent fines if forced. The general rejection of the oath of allegiance and the refusal of some to pay taxes to the new government may have been due to their radical pacifist beliefs or may have come from their opposition to the new rebel government. In any case, the Brethren were struggling with issues similar to the ones facing their twentieth-century descendants.[16]

Between The Revolutionary and The Civil Wars

In response to a brother who was advocating war on the basis of 1 Peter 2:13, 14, the Annual Meeting of 1785 offers us the first major Conference document on war. The following are excerpts from this pronouncement:

> The question arises, How far or wherein are we to submit ourselves? and this question the loving Peter may answer himself. We find (Acts 5:28) that the higher power to which Peter and John were subjects had commanded them straitly (in our German version, earnestly) that they should not teach in this name (the name of Jesus) any more, but they (the apostles) did not obey herein. And when they were asked again, "Did we not straitly command you," etc., then Peter and the apostles answered and said, "We ought to obey God rather than men."

> So we hope the dear brethren will not take it amiss when we, from all these passages of Scripture, and especially from the words of Peter, can not see or find any liberty to use any (carnal) sword, but only the sword of the Spirit, which is the word of God, by which we cast down imaginations and every high thing that exalteth itself against the knowledge of God, and bring into captivity every thought to the obedience of Christ, as Paul (2 Cor. 10:5) says.

> But that the higher powers bear the sword of justice, punishing the evil and protecting the good, in this we acknowledge them from the heart as ministers of God. But the sword belongeth to the kingdom of the world, and Christ says to his disciples: "I have chosen you from the world," etc. Thus we understand the beloved Peter, that we are to submit ourselves in all things that are not contrary to the will or command of God, and no further.[17]

It is evident that this first major Brethren Conference statement of pacifism bears the mark of traditional Anabaptist themes.

The Brethren remained firm in their opposition to participation in war during the war with England from 1812-1815 and the war with Mexico in 1845. During the second war with England, the main problem was the hardship on some Brethren families in paying fines levied for refusal to enter military service. The Conference in 1815 urged the entire congregation to bear these burdens. During the next few decades the Brethren must have had a problem with young men, who were going to muster and drill with troops. For this issue appears several times in the minutes of annual meetings. In 1822, for example, it was decided that no brother "take the liberty to go on the muster ground or take part in the festivities of Independence-day."[18] Since the fines were steep and were used to support the military, some Brethren were feeling that it was preferable to drill a few times. However, the total Brotherhood felt differently.

In 1855 a query came to the big meeting regarding the use of a weapon in self-defense. The answer denied such a right "inasmuch as the Savior says to Peter: 'Put up thy sword into his place; for all they that take the sword, shall perish with the sword.' "[19]

Brethren and The Civil War

The Brethren entered the period of the Civil War with a built-in bias. Their sympathies, for the most part, lay on the side of the Union. Most Brethren lived in the North, and those in the South wanted desperately to maintain relationships and unity in the Brotherhood. For this reason even southern Brethren opposed secession. Likewise, the Brethren had from the first opposed the slave trade and refused to accept slaveholders as members. The annual meetings from 1782 to 1863 had several times given instructions to prospective members setting forth the procedures for freeing slaves. These anti-secessional and anti-slavery sentiments led to perhaps the most supportive statement to a warring government in the history of annual meetings. Opposing the giving of special bounty-money (money given to buy a substitute) and special appeals to support the war effort, but favoring the payment of fines and taxes, the Conference of 1864 adds:

> And lest the position we have taken upon political matters in general, and war matters in particular, should seem to make us, as a body, appear to be indifferent to our government, or in opposition thereto, in its efforts to suppress the rebellion, we hereby declare that it has our sympathies and our prayers, and that it shall have our aid in any way which does not conflict with the principles of the gospel of Christ.[20]

Elder D. P. Sayler of Frederick County, Maryland, who tradition says frequently appealed the Brethren case before the War Department and on occasions was invited to the White House to pray with President Lincoln, was reported to have said at an Annual Conference at Franklin Grove, Illinois: "I have often prayed God that what he cannot do otherwise, he will do at the mouth of the cannon."[21]

Although the sympathies and prayers of all the peace churches were behind the Union cause, the Brethren did not have as many defections from their ranks as the Quakers, the Mennonites, and the Amish. Caught up in the patriotic fervor of the times, more of their youth entered the army. In all the peace churches there had been a dearth of pacifist teaching for several generations preceding the war.

In the North the pro-Union sentiments of the Brethren, the friendly attitude of President Lincoln toward conscientious objectors, the need for good farmers to produce food, and superior military strength combined to provide more comfortable exemptions for conscientious objectors than previously. At first these were provided by the laws of individual states such as Indiana and Ohio. Exempted persons were required to pay $200 in return. Later the Federal Act of 1863 provided for the hiring of substitutes or the payment of the sum of $300 for the same purpose. One year later, because of the opposition of the Society of Friends, there was greater recognition of conscience. When drafted, conscientious objectors from peace churches would be considered non-combatants and would be assigned hospital duty or responsibility for caring for freed slaves. Or they could be exempted for payment of $300. The factor, which no doubt made such payment easier, was the provision which stated that this money was to be used for the benefit of "sick and wounded soldiers" rather than the hiring of military substitutes.

In the South, the Brethren suffered more. As an isolated antislavery group, they were suspected of pro-Unionist leanings. Because of their pacifism and religious and ethnic ties with the North, they experienced various types of harassment from unfriendly neighbors. And since their farms were sometimes in the line of battle, Southern Brethren experienced the burning of barns, the destruction of crops and the killing of livestock. Some took advantage of opportunities to render deeds of mercy and offer places of refuge to the wounded. Prison and stockade experiences were common. Some Brethren and Mennonites were forced into army service against their will. Their uncooperative behavior caused some to be released consistent with the attitude of General Stonewall Jackson:

> There lives a people in the Valley of Virginia, that are not hard to bring to the army. While there, they are obedient to their officers. Nor is it difficult to have them take aim, but it is impossible to get them to take correct aim. I, therefore, think it better to leave them at their homes that they may produce supplies for the army.[22]

Other Brethren sought to meet their plight by attempting to escape either to the West or North. In March 1862, two groups of about ninety Mennonites and Dunkers fled to the West from their homes in the Shenandoah Valley of Virginia. They were captured and returned to prisons at Harrisonburg and Richmond. Examined by a representative of the War Department, they were released to their homes the next month. Because of his activities in lobbying in such situations and in securing exemptions for members, John Kline, Brotherhood leader and elder, was thrown into the guard house at Harrisonburg, Virginia, for nearly two weeks that same month.

The laws in the South had stiffer penalties and were much less consistent than in the North. Mennonite and Brethren leaders did succeed in gaining an exemption from the Virginia legislature for conscientious objectors in March 1862. The stipulation was either a payment of $500 plus two percent of the value of taxable property or serving as a teamster or in other noncombatant duties in the army. The next month, however, there was a Confederate conscription act, and the peace churches were uncertain as to their status until the next October when exemption was granted for the furnishing of a substitute or the payment of $500.

Though the Brethren set aside the subsequent New Year's Day 1863 as a day of thanksgiving, the administration of the law was not as favorable as they had hoped. In some cases hardships came when families who had paid the state of Virginia previously were now required to hand over an additional similar amount to the Confederacy. Often young men in Brethren families who had not yet been baptized were denied special exemption. During the closing years of the war, with the shortage of manpower, there was an increasing clamor against special privileges, leading finally to the order of October 8, 1864 eliminating all exemptions in the South. Such a severe blow caused Brethren again to consider leaving the South. As the war situation deteriorated, the manhunts for fugitive conscripts became more relentless. Only the surrender of General Lee in 1865 saved the Brethren from more severe persecution.

No account of the Brethren during the Civil War is complete without the story of John Kline. Though there were a few other martyrs, such as John P. Bowman, a Tennessee elder who was killed by soldiers when he pleaded with them not to take his horse, John Kline remains the "classic" martyr of this period. The story of his death is told more often than is its meaning explained. The significance of his death is related not just to his pacifist views. It stems from his determination to maintain unity in his denomination. For him the unity of the Brotherhood transcended sectional loyalties. This was consistent with his earlier views on patriotism expressed in his diary on the occasion of the Washington birthday celebrations of 1849.

> My highest conception of patriotism is found in the man who loves the Lord his God with all his heart and his neighbor as himself. Out of these affections spring the subordinate love for one's country; love truly virtuous . . . in its most comprehensive sense takes in the whole human family. Were this love universal the word patriotism, in its specific sense, meaning such a love for one's country as makes its possessors ready and willing to take up arms in its defense, might be appropriately expunged (erased) from every national vocabulary.[23]

It may have been through his efforts that a major schism was avoided. We are aware that several major American denominations were split in two as a result of the war, schisms which have only recently been healed or continue to exist to this day. John Kline crossed battle lines frequently and was repeatedly elected moderator of Annual Meeting during this period. Shortly after returning from the "great meeting" at Hagerstown, Indiana, in May 1864 he was shot dead by unidentified assassins not far from his home. He had been to a blacksmith shop and was on his way to visit a sick neighbor. His body when found had been pierced by several bullets. He was no doubt killed for his pacifist stance and his associations with "damned Yankees."

The example of their Civil War ancestors should inspire and instruct Brethren today. John Kline's enlightened patriotism which subordinated the love of country for the welfare of the entire human family should become a fundamental attitude for present Brethren in a world which has become one.

The Brethren and World War I

The Brotherhood in the last decades of the nineteenth century was more alive with many new interests than with the question of peace. The growing church spawned rival periodicals, expressed evangelistic zeal through revival meetings, supported the Sunday school movement, identified with the temperance movement, established academies and colleges, and enthusiastically sent missionaries overseas. There was a "coming out" to be more a part of mainstream American life. And there was ferment leading to a three-way schism in the 1880s over the above issues and the degree of authority of Annual Conference. The peace position was verbally affirmed before baptism and generally assumed.[24] But it was little emphasized. The decisions of Conference which were related to problems of war and peace granted permission to newly baptized members to continue receiving pensions for army service but turned down a request of veterans to attach themselves to the "Association of the Grand Army of the Republic." The Conference also turned down a proposal for active cooperation with the Peace Association of America (1875) and a later petition to send delegates to the Annual National Peace Convention (1884).

These decisions were consistent with an "Anabaptist dualism" which tended to accept taxation and pensions but to reject any activity which influenced the policies of the government. Yet at the same time it witnessed to the belief in personal nonparticipation in war. The general lack of peace teaching and activity was typical of the quietism of Brethren who seemed to be unconcerned until Brethren youth were threatened with military service. These factors contributed to the state of unpreparedness as the Brethren entered the brutal and dehumanizing twentieth century with its extensive use of torture, widespread bombings of civilians, and numerous examples of genocide.

By the beginning of the twentieth century, the Brethren began to break with their traditional stance by voting, peace resolutions, and a peace committee. Their wish was that the nation and the world might do those things which make for peace. Nevertheless, the scarce pacifist literature available for Brethren still contained an Anabaptist flavor. Such was true of the one-page tract, "Christ and War," by Daniel Vaniman:

> Christ says, "Love your enemies." War says, "Hate them."
>
> Christ says, "Do them good." War says, "Do them harm."
>
> Christ says, "Pray for them." War says, "Slay them."
>
> Christ says, "I come not to destroy men's lives but to save them."
>
> War says, "I come to destroy men's lives, and for this purpose I want the most effectual weapons that can be invented."
>
> Paul says, "If thine enemy hunger, feed him." War says, "Starve him."
>
> Paul says, "If he thirst, give him drink." War says "Destroy his wells, cut off his supplies of every kind."
>
> Paul says, "We wrestle not against flesh and blood." War says, "We do wrestle against flesh and blood. Crown them to the wall, and into the last ditch; utterly destroy them if they don't submit."[25]

The Brethren were unprepared for World War I and the government was unprepared for the conscientious objectors. The draft law of May 18, 1917, exempted such objectors from combatant service only. This meant that Brethren young men entered the army with varying advice from the Brethren leaders at home and varying treatment by army officers in the camps. They constituted a special group as they came with identification from their local boards that they were members of peace churches. As a group they were often cursed, called the vilest of names, and stood up as gazing stock for the soldiers. This was to induce them to drill and eventually to become regular combatants. Later directives from Washington discouraged this type of harassing because experience demonstrated that decent treatment was more successful in recruiting the objectors for regular army service. This remained the aim of the army throughout the war. A minority of Brethren did enter regular army service, some becoming officers.

A majority, however, accepted noncombatant service in the medical, quartermaster, or engineer corps. Quite a large group felt that any service was a part of the total effort; consequently, they refused to drill or to put on the uniform. When Secretary of War Baker visited Camp Meade and questioned a Brethren draftee, Alfred Echroth, concerning his refusal of army service of any kind, the latter said he objected to the uniform because it "would advertise militarism, the very thing we opposed . . ."[26] Such objectors were placed in detention camps with little to do except respond to various forms of harassment and perform dirty-work assignments.

In March 1918 the Farm Furlough Law was passed. Some noncombatants were released for agricultural work, the wages in excess to regular army pay going to the Red Cross. At least sixteen Brethren were placed in military prisons, most being sent to Fort Leavenworth, Kansas. I have listened to the vivid recitation by Maurice Hess, an Old Order German Baptist professor at McPherson College, of solitary confinement, a diet of bread and water, and the tying of hands to the bars of the cell. Instructions in 1918 gave permission in exceptional cases for allowing furlough service in France under the auspices of the Friends' Reconstruction Unit. Though largely Quaker, this provided a model for the later Civilian Public Service camps developed during World War II.

The confusion of the church was reflected in its leadership during World War I. Pastors and church leaders would visit the military and detention camps and give contradictory advice. Some advised the men to cooperate as much as possible, accepting noncombatant duties like hospital service. Such service and a good attitude would win more humane treatment and increasing recognition. Others advised strongly against putting on the uniform or drilling. The trying experiences of many of the young men, the growing criticism in the Brotherhood and among the drafted that the advice was unclear, and the appeals from members and districts for the church to take a stand led to the calling of a special Conference at Goshen, Indiana, January 9, 1918. Delegates were sent from districts and some local churches.

The first action of the Goshen Conference was the adoption of a resolution, to be sent to Washington, which reviewed the historic position of the church and the present unsatisfactory treatment of conscientious objectors in army camps. It requested what was not to be fully granted until World War II, namely, that drafted members be assigned noncombatant activities in agriculture and in nonmilitary industries.

The second statement defined the Brethren position on war for the use of members of the church:

> I. We believe that war or any participation in war is wrong and entirely incompatible with the spirit, example, and teachings of Jesus Christ.
> II. That we cannot conscientiously engage in any activity or perform any function contributing to the destruction of human life.[27]

On the basis of these principles, the statement commended "the loyalty of the Brethren in camps for their firm stand in not participating in the acts of war." Without criticizing those who had found work which they could conscientiously do, they appealed to them to refrain from all activity that would involve them in the arts of destruction.

The statement then went on as follows:

> We further urge our brethren not to enlist in any service which would, in any way, compromise our time-honored position in relation to war; also that they refrain from wearing the military uniform. The tenets of the church forbids military drilling, or learning the art or arts of war, or doing anything which contributes to the destruction of human life or property.[28]

The appointed Central Service Committee carried the special resolution to Washington. It was also printed, circulated widely in the churches, and given to camp visitors to carry to the men. One young man presented this statement to his officer, who relayed it to Washington. The story as it unfolds from this point is related by Roger Sappington:

> About July 8, 1918, J. M. Henry, pastor of the Church of the Brethren in Washington, D. C., and a member of the Central Service Committee of the church, was called to the office of Frederick P. Keppel, Third Assistant Secretary of War . . . Keppel read aloud a document concerning which Henry could write nearly twenty years later, "Its charges . . . still ring sometimes like a nightmare in my ears." The document "charged the officers of the Goshen Conference, and authors of the Goshen Statement, as guilty of treasonable intent of obstructing the operating of the Select Draft Law."

> . . . The other two members of the Central Service Committee were immediately called to Washington by telegram to deal with this crisis in the life of the church. After a long session together, the committee agreed to "pledge our influence and cooperation with the Church of the Brethren at large for the discontinuance of the distribution of this Statement." In Henry's words, "the Church of the Brethren was saved from the impending tragedy."[29]

From our perspective one might share the judgment of Roger Sappington that there "seems to be room for honest doubt as to whether the greater tragedy may not have been the unconditional surrender of the Brethren leaders responsible for this decision to the coercive power of the Federal government."[30]

But our role is not to repent for the mistakes of our grandfathers but to learn from them so we may be faithful in our day. Here was a direct violation of the "Espionage Law." The committee, who immediately advised the Brethren to take the paper completely out of circulation, represented a people who were just beginning to shed their religious costumes and their unpopular German identity. They wanted to be accepted. Floyd Mallott, former church historian at Bethany Theological Seminary, has conjectured that when the Brethren hopped into their first Model T Fords more than their broad-brimmed hats flew off. Their peace beliefs went as well. Many Brethren purchased Liberty Bonds. Brethren were not immune to the high degree of patriotic fervor. The peace position not only suffered erosion; it was also beginning to change in some basic ways.

Is the way of Christlike love a pattern for individual Christians only? Or might it also be a possible strategy for changing society? Should the Brethren who refuse to participate in war be more concerned to prevent wars through efforts that make for peace? That the Brethren were struggling with these questions is revealed by their actions. In 1910 a resolution of Annual Conference called on "the entire membership to activity to the cause of peace."

In 1911 a Peace Committee was appointed with the following duties:

> First: To propagate and aid in the distribution of such literature as may be helpful to the better understanding as to the sinfulness and folly of resorting to arms in the settlement of differences; Second: To use every lawful gospel means in bringing about peaceful settlements of difficulties when such may arise between governments or societies; Third: To keep the Brotherhood informed, from time to time, through our publications, as to the true status of the peace movement.[31]

Even before the war this concern for world peace was present. In the election of 1915 the usually Republican-inclined Brethren voted by a large majority for President Wilson, a Democrat, because they believed he "would keep this country out of war."[32] And in the first conference to convene after the outbreak of hostilities, the Brethren commended the Religious Educational Association of America for their resolution "to get away from pagan nationalism, to Christian internationalism."

Between the World Wars

In the decades between the two world wars the Brethren were influenced by the ecumenical movement, the growing popular peace sentiment of the twenties and thirties, and the social gospel views of liberal church leaders. The unpleasant experiences of the army camps of World War I spawned zealous peace leaders such as Dan West and M. R. Zigler. Through summer camps, caravans, work camps, Sunday schools, and the General Welfare Board, the church attempted its first programs in peace education and action. The Board of Christian Education appointed a Peace Commission which served until 1934, when the Manchester College faculty was requested to serve in this capacity.

Outside the denominational organization Dan West launched a movement in the early thirties to enlist "One Hundred Dunkers for Peace," key youth who would be trained as peace workers. These in turn would help enlist "Twenty Thousand Dunkers for Peace" to sign a pacifist pledge. Annual Conference of 1935 may have upstaged the actual execution of the plan by ambitiously adopting the slogan, "Two Hundred Thousand Dunkers for Peace."

In response to a query from the First District of West Virginia, Conference in 1934 promoted a protest movement against the payment of war taxes. Such Brethren as Kermit Eby became interested in applying their strategies of peacemaking to labor and racial disputes. The Brethren became deeply involved in relief work in Spain and China. Just prior to World War II a vision of "Brethren Service" captured the Brotherhood's imagination.

Few conferences during this period passed into history without strong pronouncements on peace. In 1922 it was advised that "members should not afflilate themselves with the American Legion or kindred ex-service organizations." In statements from 1932 to 1941 all war was declared to be sin, "unconditionally and always." Such an affirmation was new in Brethren circles. As World War II approached, the youth were advised that any form of noncombatant service was contrary to the position of the church, and the leadership was working seriously with Mennonites and Friends to secure alternative forms of service in case of another war.

Though the church was bolder, more vocal and more political in peace concerns than ever before, such activity was supported enthusiastically by a relatively small portion of the membership. Nevertheless, this increased zeal of influential Brethren leaders influenced the thinking of many members about peace. Some positions taken by the church did not eliminate but added to more traditionally held views.

The 1935 Conference at Winona Lake, Indiana, offers a case study of older Anabaptist themes mingled with newer more politically oriented ones. It declared that "war is incompatible with the spirit, example, and teachings of Jesus." Then apart from a few like references, the statement manifested a different flavor.

> We believe that war is not inevitable. Those beliefs are not based upon a peculiar peace doctrine of our own; they arise from our application of Christian standards to all human relations, whether individual, group, class, or national. To settle conflicts in any of these relationships by war is not efficient, not constructive, not permanent, and certainly not Christian. We believe that nonviolence, motivated by goodwill, is more powerful than the sword, making possible the survival of both parties, while warfare insures the ultimate destruction of both.[33]

The mixture of the old and new reflected the religious environment of the Brethren during this period. The early decades of the century saw the rise of the fundamentalist-liberal controversy. It was natural that the fundamentalist emphasis on biblical authority, the new birth, and temperance attracted many Brethren. It was also logical that many Brethren felt a kinship with liberalism, which supported a pacifist position. The liberals' belief in the "fatherhood of God" and "the brotherhood of man" and their allegiance to the Jesus of history appeared to be updated versions of historic Brethren emphases on God's love, love of neighbor and enemy, and the necessity to follow in the steps of Jesus.

Likewise, it was natural that a church which had defined religion as life, would have members attracted to the social gospel movement, which attempted to apply the message of Jesus to social, economic and political problems. Many Brethren believed in the doctrine of progress. In 1930 the publishing house released a book entitled *The Conquest of Peace*, which placed on the cover an expression of this faith: "Peace is the next great adventure for the human race. An increasing interest in the cultivation of goodwill is a sign that the blood and thunder age of man's life is past."[34] Soon the rise of Hitler and World War II would challenge this faith in progress as well as seriously test the peace church tradition.

World War II to the Present

Brethren peace views have continued to be shaped both by the gospel and by wars—in the forties, World War II; in the fifties, the United Nations war in Korea; in the sixties and early seventies, the war in Vietnam; and in the seventies and eighties, wars of liberation.

The nation and the churches saw World War II coming. Though at first there was some popular opposition to the United States' entry into the war, after Pearl Harbor in 1941 there was strong support. Because of the aggression of Hitler and Mussolini and the demonic nature of facism, World War II was widely regarded a just war. Though not promoted with the fanatical crusading spirit of World War I, it was regarded as a necessary evil to preserve freedom. The popular and large peace movement of the twenties and thirties quickly evaporated, leaving a few radical marxists and peace church remnants to offer a peace witness. When the Federal Council of Churches offically approved the war, the Mennonites withdrew. The Brethren remained to make their witness within instead of outside of conciliar circles.

As mentioned above, the peace churches were already negotiating with Selective Service for special provisions for conscientious objectors. Brethren leaders were determined not to repeat the struggles of World War I when large numbers of conscientious objectors found themselves in the armed forces. The government and the peace churches worked out an alternative called the Civilian Public Service Program, (1940-1947).

Under the provisions of the law those opposed to all military service were to be assigned "to work of national importance under civilian direction." The church began to operate a series of base camps of government-supervised work in forestry and soil conservation. Later, the government allowed CPS men to work on detached service projects at mental hospitals, in medical experimentation, and in public health and agriculture. The experiment in human starvation at the University of Minnesota and the parachuting smoke-jumper units which fought forest fires were the more sensational of these projects.

Though administered by the peace churches, the camps were open to a wide variety of conscientious objectors from marxists to Jehovah Witnesses. Some of the assignments were of doubtful worth, and this caused low morale. Additional problems came from government regulations and red tape. However, some commendable service and comaraderie came out of this arrangement. One notable legacy has been the creative institutional expressions in mental health which continue to this day.

After the war, peace church leaders were determined to devise a better system if ever again confronted with conscription. They joined others in vigorously opposing the reinstitution of the draft. The battle was lost in 1948 when Congress voted a new Selective Service law which surprisingly exempted CO's. In the same year in a dramatic move at Annual Conference, youth persuaded the delegates to institute a Brethren Volunteer Service "to serve human need . . . and the cause of peace." Brethren youth would be encouraged to give a year of their lives in Christian service.

In the Universal Military Training and Service Act of 1951, Congress required two years of civilian service by conscientious objectors but offered a much broader range of possible projects including some Brethren Volunteer Service assignments already in operation. In this way the draft, which continued through the Korean and Vietnam Wars and early seventies, constituted one of the most liberal provisions the world had ever known for objectors. The church chose, devised, and administered its own programs, which in turn were approved by the government as options among others for CO's.

In spite of the liberal provisions, some Brethren youth took a more radical stand. They shared the strong anti-war sentiments of the time. Because some draft boards refused to grant CO status to selective objectors of other traditions, a number of Brethren youth became a part of the resistance movement to conscription in any form. In 1970 the Annual Conference sanctioned their position by inserting with other revisions the following as a part of a previous statement of the Church of the Brethren on war:

> We commend to all of draft age, their parents, counselors and fellow members, the alternative positions of (1) Alternative Service as conscientious objectors engaging in constructive civilian work, or (2) open, nonviolent noncooperation with the system of conscription.
>
> The church pledges its support to the draft-age member facing conscription who chooses open noncooperation with the system of conscription as a conscientious objector. . . . All members of the church who take the position of noncooperation should seek to exhibit a spirit of humility, good-will, and sincerity in making this type of courageous witness most effective, nonviolent, and Christian.[35]

Concurrently with the above relationships with selective service the total church was engaged in a massive Brethren Service program. Following World War II the Brethren quickly launched multi-million dollar programs of relief and rehabilitation in countries devastated by war. These programs quickly involved Brethren at the grass roots. People in local communities raised heifers and other animals to send abroad, escorted the animals as seagoing cowboys, or worked as tractor drivers in special units in China. Congregations sponsored refugees, hosted foreign students, and commissioned their youth to be service workers in other countries. Brethren started or helped to start the Heifer Project, the Christian Rural Overseas Program

(CROP), the International Youth Exchange, the Brethren Service Center at New Windsor, and refugee resettlement work, including the resettlement of Japanese who were evacuated from their West Coast homes. Presently, it is estimated that three-fourths of the budget of the National Council of Churches of Christ goes for programs pioneered by Brethren leaders.

It was inevitable that such enthusiasm for service, good-will toward all, and hopes for one peaceful world would be dampened by pessimistic currents of the post-war period resulting from the growing awareness of the evil in Hitler's Germany, the impact of the Atom bomb, and the growth of totalitarianism around the world. Young people who marched from New Windsor to conquer the world through love were often disillusioned when they encountered the hard realities of entrenched evil. Concerns for justice emerged as those who were putting on so many band-aids in order to heal the world's wounds became more conscious of the sources of infection.

In the 1940s and 1950s Brethren encountered the adept critique of pacifism of Reinhold Niebuhr. We were forced to discern whether our pacifist faith was naive in its view of human progress, unrealistic in its belief in the goodness of human nature, absurd in its expectations that governments could adopt a Christ-like stance, and falsely utopian in its analyses of the future. Does a pacifist stance represent a retreat from responsible participation in political affairs?

Some Brethren have maintained their pacifism by returning to more conservative and biblical presuppositions. Repudiating both liberal and Niebuhrian desires to be effective, they argue that the calling of the Christian is to be faithful even if this leads to the way of the cross. For some this can mean a return to an Anabaptist two-kingdom posture, a political quietism which does not strive to change the state. For others it has led to a more Anabaptist counter-culture mood, a radical nonviolent posture which defines resistance as "overcoming evil with good."

Along with these neo-Anabaptist currents, many continue to embody social gospel perspectives. Others might be classi-

fied as Niebuhrians who retain strong peace and justice concerns. All of these reflect the pluralism which presently exists in
one peace church tradition. These currents will be defined more
systematically in the next chapter. The typology will not feature
the fundamental differences between pacifists and nonpacifists;
but rather the variations within the peace church tradition.

3

Variations Within the Peace Church Tradition

On the broad Kansas plains, where I grew up the churches of the Brethren were far and few between. It puzzled me that so few people had ever heard of us. When I asked my parents who we were, they said we were something like the Mennonites and Friends. From that time on I have wanted to learn more about these "peculiar" people.

The first Brethren identified consciously with the older anabaptist Mennonite movement. But very early in their history, the Brethren accepted the invitation of the Quaker, William Penn, to immigrate to Germantown. There they not only enjoyed the Quakers' beneficent rule but were influenced in polity and faith. As a result, their peace position began to develop from Anabaptist to more Quaker-like views. This development has continued and accelerated in the twentieth century.

This chapter may be too ambitious. To understand the basic motifs of the historic peace churches is to encounter both the continuities and variations of the peace church tradition as well as contemporary offshoots and kindred movements. To encompass all this is difficult, but it must be tried, for this is important background.

Mennonites

Biblicism. The Mennonite peace position traces its origin to evangelical Anabaptism which emerged as part of the radical reformation of the sixteenth century. Early statements of the Brethren show evidence of a simple biblicism, a reading of the scriptures emphasizing discipleship, obedience to the Way of Jesus and such commands as "love your enemies" and "resist not evil." I once asked Clarence Jordan, founder of the Koinonia community in Georgia, where he picked up his pacifism. He replied without hesitation: "I read the New Testament." Such could be said by Anabaptists and their descendants.

Christ Centered. Disciples are called to participate in the continuation of the love of God as demonstrated supremely in the life, death and resurrection of Jesus. A Mennonite pamphlet reasons: There are two ways Christians can approach basic issues. One is to start with the world's questions and answers. The second is to start with Christ. The first tries to give popular answers to such common questions as: What would happen if all became pacifists? Would not a Hitler or a Russia take over our country? Mennonites remind us that this is the wrong question. We need the second approach: to begin by acknowledging that Christ is Lord. What does it mean to follow Christ? How can we remain faithful to his way even though it may lead to a cross?[1]

Way of the Cross. Early Anabaptists focused on the cross as the center of their faith and life. God's way of meeting and overcoming evil in our world should be our way. "For to this you have been called, because Christ also suffered for you, leaving you an example, that you should follow in his steps" (1 Peter 2:21). If we internalize God's love even when we do not deserve it, we cannot help but love those whom we judge to be unworthy of our love. Unlike most of Christendom, Mennonites have not separated the doctrine of the atonement from the biblical commandment to love enemies.

Shalom Life Style. Such grace then penetrates the total life style of Christians. We manifest the first fruits of the Kingdom of peace and justice in mutual aid and love within the community of faith. In this way we point to the love which God wills for the entire world.

Religious Freedom. The peaceful wing of Anabaptism repudiated any coercion or manipulation of faith by the state in favor of the principle of voluntaryism in matters of religion. Therefore, they refused to use the sword either to impose their will on others or to defend themselves. This led them also to refuse to participate in offices which sanctioned the use of the sword. Though the Mennonite posture has often been non-participation, in times when they have been free from the terror of persecution, they have participated in nonviolent functions of the state.

A Kingdom Ethic. The Anabaptists have an eschatological (end time) or kingdom ethic. We are to live now as if the kingdom has already come, even in a world more realistically characterized as a kingdom of darkness. Anabaptists are a pilgrim people who live in the world yet have their real citizenship in a kingdom which is both partly present and yet to come in fulness. In their life together Anabaptists experience and point to some first fruits of the kingdom coming. Such was the witness of a Mennonite conscientious objector in Russia. He was brought before a judge who chided him about the impractability of his stand. "Do you not realize that the kingdom has not yet come?" To this the youth replied: "For you, judge, and for Russia, the kingdom may not have yet come. But it has come for me and I must begin to live now in this reality."

Positive and Negative Evaluations

The Anabaptist stance takes into account the inability of worldly wisdom to calculate consequences in a complicated world and finds its power in the singleminded purpose to follow Jesus. Gordon Kaufman, a Mennonite theologian states it well:

> Nonresistance is not based on any pragmatic conviction that it will win the war or melt the hearts of the enemy or anything else of that sort; it is based on the eschatological (future oriented) conviction at the very heart of the Christian faith that the future is in Jesus Christ and that therefore we can accept whatever that future might bring without regard for ourselves, even though it bring a cross.[2]

Because it is identified with the cross, the peace position is not an appendage of the faith but is at the heart of it. Anabaptists call the community of faith to experience the first fruits of the kingdom of peace now. "Let peace begin with me," as the words of the song go (though *us* would be a more Anabaptist rendition). But the price of the way of peace may be suffering love. That biblical realism is an often needed corrective to the many popular success theologies of our time.

But those who teach the nonresistant way often translate pacifism (peacemaking) as passivism. They stress the command to "resist not evil" and neglect the call to "overcome evil with good." They lack a sense of mission to the structures and powers of the world. They emphasize almost exclusively the Lordship of Christ over the individual. When this teaching combines with lower expectations for society and the state, it is easy to neglect the message of the prison epistles that Christ is Lord over all. Teaching too exclusively the theology of the cross minimizes the theology of resurrection. Strong demands for obedience combine with expectations of suffering to present the Christian way as a heavy burden. Children of Anabaptism need not abandon their discipleship theology, but they often need a strong dose of a theology of grace when they fall short of their high expectations.

Quakers

The Quaker peace testimony emerged as a part of the radical reformation in England. The awakening of George Fox occurred near the middle of the seventeenth century.

Holy Spirit. The Quakers might be called the charismatics of the peace tradition. A belief in the presence, power and authority of Jesus Christ through the Spirit is the starting point for their peace testimony. In a declaration to Charles II in 1661, Friends attributed their stand to "the Spirit of Christ, which leads us into all truth and will never move us to fight and war against any man with outward weapons, neither for the Kingdom of Christ nor for the Kingdoms of this world."[3]

Presence of the Seed of Christ. The Friends believe the seed of Christ to be present in all people. "The true light that enlightens every man was coming into the world" (John 1:9). Because of the presence of Christ and the witness of the Holy Spirit in all people, Quakers have been more open to the possibilities of the kingly rule of Christ or the work of the Spirit outside the community of faith. Though the witness of the Inward Christ is reinforced by the New Testament portrait of Jesus' overcoming evil by the power of love, Scriptures have authority because of the continual presence of Christ who is both author and authoritative interpreter of the Bible. And the living Christ continues to be present within the community to take away the hatred and pride which provide the occasion for war.

Charismatic Transformationalists. Light has been a favorite biblical word for Friends. The light not only signifies Christ's presence overcoming sin within our hearts, but also the establishment of Christ's rule in human society. For Quakerism there is not one Lord for the church and a Lord who requires lesser things from others. There is only one kingdom under the Lordship of Christ. Fox was very much in the Puritan tradition in his desire to transform not only the church but the entire society so that it might be ruled by God's love.

But Fox was not like many radical Puritans who wanted to accomplish this by taking over and ruling from the top. The early Quakers shared the radical apocalypticism of their period, the expectation of a powerful expression of the Spirit breaking into the present. As charismatics live with a sense of expectancy of God's gifts empowering individuals, Quakers believe the leading and power of the Spirit can miraculously usher in manifestations of justice, peace and righteousness.

Lamb's War. Christ wants to enlist his people to fight now in the Lamb's War, a metaphor which is found in the Book of Revelation. The Lamb's War is an eternal, prophetic, missionary, evangelistic, ideological, social, economic and political struggle against evil in human history until god in mercy brings history to the peaceable kingdom promised by Isaiah and described in Revelation. This war, however, is waged with the nonviolent loving weapons symbolized by the Lamb. For this struggle we need to be open to the perfecting of our lives by the Holy Spirit in the confidence that the Lord is at work in this thick night of darkness.

Positive and Negative Evaluations

Some are saying that in our present situation no one belongs in the peace movement who does not believe in miracles. By this standard Friends really are in, for they are convinced that God can do something through and with their witness on behalf of peace and justice. The belief that God's image or Christ's seed is given to all has nurtured a humanitarian concern for the needs and rights of all races and nationalities. The conviction that the way of Christ is for everyone has often given them boldness to preach the gospel of peace to everyone, including those in power. And their Spirit theology has often empowered them with a spirituality which joins the inward journey of prayer with the outward journey of peacemaking.

But the point of strength is often the place of weakness. The faith of the Friends in the transforming power of the Spirit can be accompanied by a naive optimism which refuses to recognize the entrenched nature and depth of evil. The affirmation that there is something of God in every person can evolve into a naive faith in the natural goodness of humanity negating the need for God's redeeming activity. The mystical sense of being led by Christ can lead to an attitude of absolute certainty about God's will which may seem arrogant and inflexible to others. And the zealous desire to improve society may lead to false identifications of our favorite ideologies and causes with the kingdom of God.

Brethren

The Brethren peace tradition may be at the same time more simple and more difficult to describe. More simple because the position can be defined in relationship to the Mennonites and Quakers, but more difficult because of its less distinctive nature.

Anabaptist. We have noted how early Brethren statements on peace and war have a strong Anabaptist flavor. They are rooted in the Bible and they stress discipleship. The Brethren have been described by others as a community of people attempting to live according to the Sermon on the Mount. In 1785 the Brethren yearly meeting declared: "We cannot see or find any liberty to use the sword, but only the sword of the spirit, the Word of God." Even today, Brethren often look to Mennonites such as John H. Yoder for biblical interpretations which undergird old foundations and shed new light on contemporary issues.

Quaker and Pietist Influences. The Pietist milieu of "heart" religion anticipated a radical historical manifestation of the Spirit of peace. By the nineteenth and twentieth centuries this sometimes latent theme emerged as the Brethren moved to a transformationist stance, with the stress on making society more Christian. Their political interests and service programs came to be modeled more after the style of the Quakers.

Ecumenical. There has been a style of peacemaking within the church which no doubt influenced the more outward peacemaking efforts. Historically the Brethren have manifested an eagerness to "maintain the unity of the Spirit in the bond of peace" (Eph. 4:3). Though not always successful, the Brethren have worked hard to stay together. The focus has been on relationships, unity, reconciliation and love. Historians of the civil rights movement have discovered that the best record we have of the events at Selma, Alabama in 1965 is the diary of Brethren Ralph Smeltzer who was moving from one group to another in an effort to bring the opposing sides together. The cooperative side of the more churchly Brethren has served as a catalyst in stimulating peacemaking efforts within other traditions and the conciliar movement.

Positive and Negative Evaluations

Brethren peacemakers, from time to time, have sought to combine the strengths of the Mennonite and Quaker traditions. They envision a style which holds together the faithfulness to the way of the cross of the Mennonites with the more active and optimistic stance of the Quakers. In this vision it is possible for the peace witness to embody both nonresistance and loving resistance. To the picture of Jesus as one who "when he was reviled . . . did not revile in return, when he suffered, he did not threaten" (1 Pet. 2:23) might be added the story of how he overturned the tables in the temple. Applied to church-state relationships, this posture means there is neither a naive expectation that the state will become Christian nor an acceptance of a lesser ethical norm for secular governments. The witness is loving, yet bold; evangelical, yet political; nonconformist, yet involved, leaving the question of relevance in the hands of God. I intend to put more flesh on this vision in subsequent chapters.

For the most part, the Brethren have failed to articulate their vision or visions clearly enough to be understood. Both the Anabaptist and Quaker views come through with greater clarity. Many have difficulty understanding the basis for Brethren peacemaking. Rather, the genius of the Brethren has been their practical programs and institutional contributions. For example, in offering their service centers as a place for ministries of Church World Service, the Brethren have been willing to give up the Brethren identity of these programs and relinquish them to the larger church.

The pluralism of the Brethren can be described as an invigorating synthesis. Negatively, it can be called confusion. In reality the tension which is present in the meeting of two strands leads to either creative expressions or divisive coalitions. Furthermore, efforts to stay together are open to criticism. To some, the Brethren seem more concerned with unity than with truth. At Selma the attempts at reconciliation were regarded by many as an unwillingness to identify with the oppressed. And this reconciling and cooperative stance has meant that the peace position of the Brethren has been more subject to acculturation and erosion.

Political Pacifism

As a boy I learned that Jesus was a pacifist. To follow him was to be against war. This was Anabaptism. But the notion of pacifism first came alive for me through political pacifism. Philosophers call this utilitarian or consequential pacifism, where one believes pacifism will result in the greatest good for the greatest numbers. A better name might be practical or pragmatic pacifism. This view may be a possible outgrowth of or kindred stance to certain Quaker expressions. It would be wrong, however, either to credit or to blame the followers of Fox for the rise of political pacifism in the first half of the twentieth century.

Attending a work camp in the slums of my own city, I was baptized into political pacifism by a brilliant young seminarian from Yale, Ernest Lefever. The Jesus way of peacemaking was proclaimed as a practical possibility in international affairs. The only trouble with this was that it had never been tried. My first sermon was entitled "Christianity Works." It was full of success stories gathered from personal experiences and from the lives of heroes of goodwill. From college days I can recall bull sessions in which we dreamed of the positive possibilities of bombing Berlin with Buicks and bananas and other good things.

My own adolescent pacifism was a less sophisticated version of the education materials, conference resolutions and official documents of peace church literature at that time, especially from the Brethren and Friends. A popular Brethren preacher wrote in 1958: "We shall proclaim with the reformer's zeal the dramatic possibilites in nonresistance, goodwill, reconciliation and resolute love in the practical and political affairs of mankind."[4]

Since political pacifism has been a dominant strand in pacifist theology in the twentieth century, it is important to examine

its background and basic themes. It has been said that Mennonites prayed while Brethren voted to keep Quakers in office,
though all the plain people were interested in a more beneficent
government and a better society. They returned in subsequent
generations to a stricter Anabaptist posture of nonparticipation in
the affairs of government. They regarded voting and holding
office as participating in the use of the sword. When prohibition
came, however, the Puritan desire to bring society under the laws
of God helped condition Mennonites and Brethren for greater
participation in the affairs of the state. By 1918 the Annual Conference of the Brethren were allowing that in a democracy "it is
not wrong for brethren to serve their communities and munici-
palities to promote efficiency and honesty in social and civic
life, when the nonresistant principle and the New Testament doctrine on oaths are not violated."[5]

The peace churches were influenced in varying degrees by
liberal and social gospel motifs. The love theology of the peace
churches seemed similar to liberal proclamations of God's love
and the brotherhood of man. The historic emphasis on imitating
Christ seemed to be supported by the liberal quest for the historical Jesus. The kingdom emphasis of their radical heritage was
echoed in the social gospel theology of Walter Rauschenbusch.

Many moved beyond the faith of the historic peace churches
and adopted a more humanistic view of human nature, the doctrine of progress and the calling of all to join in building the
kingdom of God on earth.

Critique. With the impact of two world wars, a great depres-
sion, holocausts in Germany and Hiroshima, and increasing
totalitarianism, peace church folk began to see that the doctrine
of progress was more a personal hope than a description of reality. When political pacifists encountered the problems and the
depth of evil as the twentieth century continued, they often
became disillusioned. Their pacifism no longer seemed so practical. This skepticism was a part of my own pilgrimage. Like
Soren Kierkegaard, I discovered that love does not always elicit

love. Rather, love may provoke evil reactions. For we often hate a good, loving person who shows us up for who we really are. The most loving man who ever lived was not successful in winning over his enemies. Instead, they nailed him to a cross.

In the decades following World War II pacifists had to deal with critiques such as Reinhold Niebuhr's. He had been chairman of the religious pacifist Fellowship of Reconciliation. But he rejected pacifism because of his own experiences as a pastor in Detroit. Identifying with the auto workers in their struggles against Ford, Neibuhr came to feel that justice required more than love. In many cases force is necessary in order to keep a greater evil from triumphing. He felt that moral choices were between shades of gray and that pacifists, by attempting to remain pure, retreated from more effective action. Responsible decisions might involve the necessity to compromise one's refusal to use coercive violence.

Some peace church leaders followed Niebuhr and turned their backs on their own tradition when they became convinced that pacifism was no longer an effective strategy for world peace and the wave of the future. Other peace church pilgrims dealt with the crisis by critiquing the presupposition of effectiveness held by both political pacifists and Niebuhrian realists. The real question they said, is not "Will it work?" Instead for the Christian it is "What is the way of Christ?" Many reworked their position to include this Anabaptist corrective to political pacifism.

Today it is surprising to observe the return of this mood of pragmatic pacifism. We find ourselves in the kind of world in which pacifism seems to be the only viable and sensible alternative. Perhaps the answer can be found in what my brother, Kenneth Brown, has named a "rule pacifism." Such comes from the recognition that our kind of world is so complex that we cannot know the consequences of our actions. The mistake of realists is that they judge the way of the cross to be mistaken on the basis of immediate results. A more long-range perspective is set forth in the following affirmations:

1. God is concerned with the welfare of the creation, including those beings created in God's image.

2. The revelation in Christ, the way of the cross, as a supreme act of God and revelation of his will, is not inconsistent with this end.

3. The pacifist need not disregard concern for consequences, but has faith that God's answer to evil—the cross—does result in the lesser of evils and that the following of the way of Christ is that which leads to the eventual welfare of all.[6]

Humanist Pacifism

Humanist pacifism may simply be defined as the refusal to destroy life because human life is regarded as sacred. Many expressions are similar to those found in Quaker circles. If there is truly something of God in every person, one should refuse to murder God. In spite of the doctrine of the fall, the image of God is not entirely destroyed. Otherwise it would be impossible for any one to respond to the saving activity of God.

Critique. The peace churches have produced many who exemplify Elton Trueblood's category of cut-flowers. Nurtured in a community which featured Jesus as a man for others, they have retained strong humanitarian concerns even when they have separated from their religious roots. These people might have been seen as an admirable contribution to the larger society until the more recent attacks on secular humanism.

Historically, humanism has been used to describe the new enhancement of men and women, which came at the time of the Renaissance when the culture and literature of ancient Greece and Rome were recovered. There were pagan and Christian expressions of humanism. Christian humanists gave us more accurate biblical texts as a result of the recovery of ancient culture. More technically "humanism" can refer to any philosophy which places our ultimate faith in human beings. The peace church tradition joins others in rejecting such assumptions.

But inasmuch as the word refers to humanitarian concerns for the welfare of all peoples, it should be stressed that Christianity at its best does not oppose humanism. A religion which places a Person at the center of its faith, instead of a book, rules, an idea or an institution, offers a heritage that declares the supreme worth of each person. At its best Christianity does not oppose reverence and concern for life. Rather, it offers a sounder foundation.

If we love people because they are naturally lovable, when they are found to be unlovely we may lose our idealism and be counted with disillusioned liberals. On the other hand, if the foundation for our love is the affirmation that God loves them, then we can go right on loving even when they are unlovely. If we accept people because of their potentiality, we will be disillusioned when they fail to become responsible. If we accept people because we know we have been accepted by God even when we are unacceptable, we will grow in grace so as to accept those whom we regard as unacceptable.

It should not be possible to sing about Christ's dying for us while we were sinners and at the same time to assert individually: "I deserve to be where I am because I have worked hard. Why should I feel sorry for the lazy bums in the slums or the peasants in Central America." Neither a Christian nor a humanist would support this deficiency in grace. Christians should never put down genuine humanitarian concerns; for God's Spirit of love can blow wherever it wills. As Christians, however, we are aware that our love of others is rooted deeply in God's impartial love for all of us.

Church-World Dualism

During the Vietnam war a group of youth were visiting with an old elder of a Canadian Anabaptist group. He emphasized that his own church held firmly to the nonresistant way. No member of his community would be found in battle. At the same time, he was pleased that Yankee soldiers were fighting in Asia to protect all of us from the evil forces of communism. His stance represents a logical extension of what has been called church-world dualism. The roots can be traced back to the six-teenth century.

Generally there was widespread acceptance of aspects of Luther's two kingdom theology in Anabaptist circles. They agreed with Luther's pessimistic analysis of the restraining function of the state. Because of the fall, God in mercy approves the use of the sword to keep people from destroying each other. Luther preached that in personal relations Christians should live the way of the Sermon on the Mount. In their political life, however, they were called to participate in the coercive functions of the worldly orders of creation. Luther's view has been called the doctrine of two kingdoms. The Anabaptists' view of the "now, not yet," nature of the kingdom often carries the same two kingdom label, but it is not as appropriate for them. Their dualism was between the present age and the age to come. Unlike Lutherans, Anabaptists could not conscientiously participate in the violent coercive functions of the state. Since they rejected the summons to participate in two kingdoms at the same time, their view is better named a church-world dualism.

Today, many peace church Christians adhere to this stance. This is the view defined in pamphlets of the Brethren Revival Fellowship. It holds that the kingdom and methods of Christ are not of this world. For this reason Christ's disciples will not fight (John 18:36). But God permits Caesar to do some things the church cannot do. God has ordained the state to punish evil and protect the good.

It is in this context that pacifism is rejected. It is regarded by some as Satan's counterfeit for the doctrine of nonresistance. Pacifists are those who believe in the innate goodness of human nature and the doctrine of progress. They are determined to change the world according to their own humanistic notions. Nonresistant Christians, however, adhere to the principle of the separation of church and state. The mission of the church is to preach the gospel and save souls from the fallen world to become members of the redeemed community. Nonresisters abide by the biblical injunctions to pay taxes and be good citizens. On the other hand, pacifist resisters are accused of disobeying the biblical command to "resist not evil," through attempts to coerce the state by refusing taxes and other manipulative tactics.

Critique. Positively, this position is often called biblical realism, a recognition of the extent and depth of the demonic. This expression of Anabaptism understands with Niebuhr that governments which serve the basic self-interests of their people will not readily turn the other cheek. Those who adhere to a church-world dualism rightly call us to preach the gospel of repentance to individual Christians. Their criticism of the arrogance and violent-prone activity of peace activists is often valid. And they keep before us a praiseworthy biblical paradigm, namely, the moving example of those who prefer to endure suffering rather than to inflict suffering.

Yet, is it biblical to espouse a dualistic ethic, one standard for the individual Christian, a lesser ethic for the state? Does such a stance make Christ Lord over the church and fail to assert the biblical claim that Christ is Lord over the world? Are we called to participate with Christ in disarming the powers and principalities (Col. 2:15)? Though it is naive to expect noble behavior of unredeemed humanity, we may nevertheless, be called to weep with Jesus in hoping that present Jerusalems might know the things that make for peace? Are we not called to preach repentance to the Ninevehs of our day? Might an exclusive emphasis on "resist not evil" overlook the Pauline admonition "to overcome evil with good"? Furthermore it has often been observed that a sharp dualism between the church and the world can easily lead to self-righteousness which fails to discern the Spirit of Christ in the world or the presence of the fallen world in the church.

Yes, we are called to preach the gospel persuasively and powerfully. Such proclamation can be in deed as well as word, even through public liturgical acts that dramatize God's no to death and God's yes to life. Are we not called to preach the gospel to all the world, including those in high places? And we can too easily forget that preaching the gospel to individuals in church can be as coercive and manipulative as public prayer vigils and sit-ins at the Pentagon.

The fact is that the early Anabaptists found it difficult to adhere to a strict church-world dualism. They affirmed the legitimate need for punishment for the sake of order, but when the hangman's noose was placed around their necks, they appealed to the state to be more Christian. The first Anabaptist community marched through the streets of Zurich wearing willow twigs or ropes, crying, "Woe, Woe! Woe to Zurich" in order to protest an action of the Town Council. At various times Mennonites have appealed to the state to support prohibition, protect conscience, eliminate conscription, and settle disputes through arbitration. Some nonresistant Mennonites have approved of capital punishment. But in the sixties Mennonites began to affirm that there are not two norms, one for the church and one for the state, but one norm for the entire world, Jesus Christ. And in applying this they declared that capital punishment is wrong not only for the Christian but also for the state.[7]

Vocational Pacifism

Reinhold Niebuhr, mentioned previously because of his critique of political pacifism, also popularized the idea of vocational pacifism. When he turned away from his pacifist stance, he, nevertheless, still maintained that Jesus was a pacifist of the nonresistant type. He argued that the way of suffering love is at the heart of the New Testament message, though if one desires to be responsible and relevant, Niebuhr added, it is not possible to follow this way of absolute love. But the ideal expression of love we have in Jesus is still important, for in making the necessary choices and compromises necessary to attain justice, pure love serves as a standard which helps determine which is the lesser of two evils. So it is with the continual incarnation of this love in history. Pure pacifist types are needed to serve as living examples of the way of suffering love. Such witnesses fill a valuable role guiding those working in society in making the right decisions.

Niebuhr felt that it was the vocational calling of some to adopt such a role. He approved the witness of the Mennonites, who were satisfied to model this way in their communities without attempting to convert all of society to the same. He was more critical of the Quakers, who wanted to universalize this love, even pressuring policy makers in Washington to become pacifists.

Major strands of the peace church tradition have advocated vocational pacifism for the church. The entire community of faith was to renounce the use and spirit of the sword as much as possible. But such behavior was not to be expected of society as a whole. It was logical that many church-world dualists appropriated Niebuhr's congenial analysis.

The spirit of individualism in the twentieth century has produced another expression of vocational pacifism within the peace church tradition. This view maintains that the community should respect the consciences of those who choose the military as well as those who decide to become conscientious objectors. It might be helpful to examine this kind of vocational pacifism against the background of the statement on "the Church and Conscription," adopted by the Church of the Brethren Annual Conference in 1957.

> We declare again that our members should neither participate in war nor learn the art of war.
>
> It is recognized, however, that not all our members will hold the beliefs which the church recommends. Some will feel conscientiously obligated to render full military service and others noncombatant military service. Some, on the other hand, may feel compelled to refuse even to register under a conscription law. Since the church desires to maintain fellowship with all who sincerely follow the guidance of conscience, it will respect such decisions, in spite of its disappointment that its message has not been taught better or comprehended more fully. It will extend its prayers, spiritual nurture, and material aid to all who struggle and suffer for a fuller understanding of God's will.[8]

It is obvious that the above statement does not give a rationale for vocational pacifism. Rather, it calls for the adoption of the pacifist position by all of its members while expressing an attitude of disappointment but support for those who conscientiously depart from the beliefs of the church. Nevertheless, there has been a growing tendency by peace church members and congregations to approve whatever a member in good conscience decides on issues of war and peace. This mood is often accompanied by the congregations' neglect to proclaim and teach publicly its traditional opposition to participation in war.

Critique. This vocational pacifism is based on a pervasive mood of relativism, the philosophy that moral judgments vary with individuals and environments. Such a philosophy can be a part of a Christian's loving understanding of why persons act and behave as they do. To relativize our norms, however, is more an expression of American individualism than a desire to be faithful to the Way. Vocational pacifism may be more the result of accommodating the militarism of our culture than of genuine tolerance. Some of its strongest advocates would not show the same degree of tolerance on other issues. The same persons would not be led to say: "Sisters and brothers, some of you may decide to become prostitutes, to get drunk, or to commit adultery. If this results from the leading of your conscience, we want you to know that we approve what you do."

The Niebuhrian and church-world bases for vocational pacifism is more difficult to critique. From the author's bias, this position has more integrity. In light of the critique of church-world dualism, it is not necessary to repeat similar pro and con reactions.

In some congregations we find yet another expression of vocational pacifism. The common double standard attitudes in relationship to pastors take shape around this issue. Since our peace heritage is an ideal, it should be espoused and lived by our leaders whether the rest of us can buy it or not. One senses that the pastor is paid to be a pacifist, to model an ideal which the rest of us want to keep but cannot enthusiastically espouse because either of fear or doubt. Such attitudes may represent a contemporary form of the dual moral ethics of the Middle Ages which considered the perfection of Christ to be only for the "religious" who were primarily in monastic orders. A lesser ethic could be expected from other Christians. For the peace church tradition, such a scheme violates the strong bias that all believers are called to be disciples of Christ and ministers in the world.

Selective Pacifism - Nuclear Pacifism

In his address before an international peace gathering in Budapest in September 1984, Professor Paolo Ricca, a Waldensian from Italy, affirmed the theme of the gathering, "Toward a Theology of Peace." He pleaded for the reversal of the historical separation between theology and peace in the Christian tradition. He claimed that theologians have worked more to justify war than to produce a theology of peace. Why is it, he pointed out, that even in Christian countries conscientious objectors have had to justify themselves and explain why they have refused war. But youth taking the oath for military duty have not had to give their reasons for accepting war.

His address was heard gladly by peace church ears. But in all fairness, the peace churches have known a more positive experience in recent years. Sizable numbers of Christians from just war traditions have become selective pacifists. It has been the experience of the peace churches that the just war theory was employed by theologians to justify every war which came along. Recently, however, the application of the just war criteria has led to a decided no to present and contemplated wars. This was especially the case in judgments about Vietnam. The same consciousness, whether informed by the criteria of the just war tradition or not, has generated increasing numbers of nuclear pacifists, those who could approve many past wars while repudiating all planning and participation in nuclear war.

The classical theory of ancient Greece and Rome required that a war defend justice and restore peace in order for it to be just. Such a war had to be fought under the authority of the state and in good conduct. Augustine added the motivation of Christian love. Since love is an inward disposition, he reasoned that it was possible to love and to kill at the same time in order to have a better society. Throughout history additional requirements have been added. War must be the only remaining means of achieving justice. The justice of the cause must involve self-defense. There must be reasonable hope for victory. The war must be executed by lawful authority. Innocent people must not be killed. The military action must be as limited as possible. Atrocities and reprisals are excluded. Above all, the good to be achieved must outweigh the probable evil effects of the war.

Critique. It is easy for peace church proponents to give pat criticisms, even of those who apply the above just war criteria and become pacifists in reference to a particular war. For peace church advocates believe that the weight of the biblical message declares all wars are sin. Since the decision for pacifism in reference to a particular war is based on practical considerations instead of biblical imperatives, a further critique of selective pacifism might follow closely the critique of political pacifism. A telling analysis was made by a Roman Catholic of his own tradition. James Douglass is convinced that a doctrine which emerged to give reasons for war cannot adequately provide the basis and power for an antiwar stance:

> It is evident that the doctrine [of a just war] is too weak in its theological presuppositions to be able to support the cross, either the cross of conscientious objection or the cross of unilateral disarmament. The foundations of a just-war theory do not have the strength to sustain adequately the kind of witness demanded today by its own moral logic, which taken by itself compels one to relinquish all recourse to modern war.[9]

Nevertheless, Mennonites, Quakers and Brethren feel close to selective and nuclear pacifists. We agree that wars, nuclear or non-nuclear, which are presently on the drawing boards, are immoral. We can join with a loud amen when selective pacifists prophetically preach that it is a sin to make a nuclear weapon. It is foolish to allow our debates about past wars to divide us. Furthermore, we "old" pacifists must confess that in witnessing to the state we often use just war criteria to call the state to live up to its own stated purposes. These same principles have meant that in spite of our rejection of all wars we have been more emotionally against some wars than others.

Some of our youth were drawn into close relationships with selective objectors during the long period of the post-World War II draft. I was led to a strong personal empathy for their special situation. Draftees, who opposed all wars, were favored with special provisions for alternative service, but those who objected to a particular war were not. Draft boards refused to grant them the status of conscientious objectors. This led some to suggest that such favored treatment of one kind of religious CO over another violates the constitutional provision against favoring one religion.

Many peace church members imbibed a strong prejudice against draft evaders or resisters during the Vietnam period. They seemed not to comprehend the predicament of the selective conscientious objector who came to this position through the application of his own religious heritage. Because of the refusal of the government to grant the CO status, the draftee was faced with only three options: fight in an immoral jungle war half way around the world, emmigrate to countries like Canada or Sweden, or resist by disobeying the law. Seeing how they were trapped by these unacceptable options makes the objectionable and emotional behavior of some more understandable.

A number of Mennonites, Friends and Brethren gave up their favored status and became resisters themselves out of a sense of identification with their comrades whose CO claims had been denied by draft boards. It is unlikely that governments will ever grant equal status to selective objectors. Practically, the compulsory draft would be undercut if each youth were allowed to determine the justice of each particular war. Members of congress have pointed out that it is not difficult to estimate the number of absolute pacifists from the peace churches and other groups, but if selective conscientious objection were allowed, it would confuse the situation and make planning difficult. Precisely because of the lack of official sanction for selective pacifists, the peace churches should be especially supportive of those who are faithfully attempting to follow the just war teachings of their own tradition.

It is difficult to gain a clear understanding of pacifism by looking at the many variations which exist among those who willingly or unwillingly carry this label. Some may protest that such a typology confuses more than it clarifies. The purpose of this chapter, however, has been to engage in dialogue with the various stances to help test our call to peacemaking.

There is something to the observation that diversity and infighting among the lovers of peace seems to undermine the power of a unified witness. But there are continuities as well as discontinuities in peace church perspectives. With the New Call to Peacemaking there are increasing areas of agreement. These common themes include basing peacemaking on biblical and spiritual foundations, maintaining the historic call to discipleship as a central motif in peace church theology, retaining a call to follow our Lord in cross-bearing, emphasizing resurrection hope and kingdom theology, cultivating an ecclesiology in which peacemaking must be a part of the internal life of the community, combining a servant theology with increasing concerns for justice, featuring the ministry of reconciliation, calling for primary allegiance to Christ as the best service to render to the state, and engaging in prophetic witness to the world. As this chapter has featured the differences, the exploration of biblical foundations in the next chapter will convey these common themes.

4

Biblical Themes for Peacemaking

Pacifists have often marshaled as many biblical texts as possible in order to "wipe out" the arguments of their opponents. Some who are not so likely to look to the Bible for authority in other areas often become avid biblicists in this one. To many conservatives, political pacifists often appear to be hypocritical in their selective use of the Bible. On the other side, peace church Christians observe that many defenders of biblical authority rely almost entirely on secular and humanistic arguments about the communist menace and the virtues of democracy in order to make their case for a strong military defense.

The peace churches believe peacemaking to be rooted in biblical faith. It is not the purpose of this chapter, however, to gather a great amount of textual support for pacifism or attempt to deal in detail with problematic passages. Other writers have done this well and I particularly recommend books by G. H. C. Macgregor and Dale Aukerman.[1] The intent of this chapter is to look at fundamental biblical themes for peacemakers.

Creation and Fall

A basic biblical affirmation appears in the last verse of the first chapter of the Bible: "God saw everything that had been made and behold it was very good." The Judeo-Christian tradition has a high view of creation. As an adolescent I was taken to a play produced by blacks. it was called "Green Pastures." It told the story of creation. The most vivid impression which stayed with me is the picture of God strutting around heaven dressed to a T. God would create something. This would rise from the floor, and a low bass voice would boom: "That's good." Finally male and female emerged and God exclaimed: "That's good, baby; that's very, very good!"

This strong affirmation of the goodness of creation is not universal. In some religious and philosophical views, the fall is equated with creation. Instead of coming later, the fall occurs whenever anything emerges that is other than spiritual, which may be defined as invisible and nonmaterial. When anything becomes earthly or fleshly, you have something less than spiritual.

My grandfather told about the first time an old Brethren elder in Oklahoma tasted ice cream. His first reaction was: "Anything that tastes this good has to be of the devil." The old elder articulated a kind of dualism which regards anything pleasurable, fun, fleshly or material as un- or anti-spiritual. This is not the kind of dualism in Paul's contrast between living in the spirit and walking in the flesh (Gal. 5:16-24). To live in the spirit is to live in proper relationship with our Creator and all of creation. To walk in the flesh is to walk in ways which violate God and others and misuse God's good material creation. Paul's lists of works of the flesh and of fruit of the Spirit both include attributes often regarded as "spiritual" and "fleshly."

Redemption

If the world as created was good, God desires to redeem not destroy the creation. A nuclear holocaust is not part of the plan of God. And God's children are called to participate in God's redeeming activity. It is true that major groups within the peace church tradition appropriated "love not the world" texts to support separatist stances over against fallen structures. These existed, however, along side this-worldly efforts to be proper stewards of God's good earth, to care for refugees and others in need, and to model love for neighbors and enemies.

One way to define the fall is to say human beings make a bad use of a good thing. In a world that spends over one and one-half million dollars each minute for weapons of death, we need to name such gross misuse of the good earth for what it is—namely, blasphemy against the goodness of God's creation.

In his book on the creation and fall, Dietrich Bonhoeffer interprets the fall as the destruction of right relationships with other human beings as well as God.[2] This has been a traditional interpretation of the peace churches. According to popular preachers, we should be willing to name and have named our individual sins. But if these preachers were to move beyond these to name the sins we commit together, the flow of money would cease. Isaiah cried out even against the aquisition of defensive weapons: "Woe to those who go down to Egypt for help and rely on horses, who trust in chariots because they are many and in horsemen because they are very strong, but do not look to the Holy One of Israel or consult the Lord!" (31:1). Can we dare be less prophetic in our situation?

Redemption—The Holy War Tradition. The biblical story is the story of the redemption of God's people. The Exodus event is central. It tells of the blessings and unfaithfulness of the chosen people in responding to God's promises to bring them out of Egypt into the promised land. Bloody wars engineered, blessed, and fought by God were a part of this story. Pacifists can neither deny nor neatly explain away the presence of the Holy War tradition in the Old Testament. Peace church members have often been tempted by the heresy of Marcion. He rejected the Old Testament because its God of wrath did not measure up to the loving God of Luke and Paul. For the most part teachers of the peace tradition have avoided this temptation. There has been a growing awareness that the Old Testament was the sacred book of the early Christians, that it is impossible to properly interpret the gospel apart from understanding the story of Israel, and that one finds themes of wrath and love, law and grace, despair and hope, in both Testaments.

Scholars have been busy interpreting the Holy War texts and the problem of war in the Old Testament. For some the early wars of Israel offer a biblical paradigm for contemporary liberation struggles of oppressed peoples. Norman Gottwald in his massive work, *The Tribes of Israel*,[3] documents this particular view. The holy war tradition, according to this analysis, can be used to justify the violence of the poor, but not the massive armaments of the superpowers. There are scholars who stress the realism of the biblical writers who tell it like it was or is.[4] The sins of God's heroes and people are not whitewashed. Though war is immoral, God can work through violence to achieve divine purposes.

Mennonite scholar Millard Lind represents those who interpret the war texts as miracle stories.[5] The recitation of God's mighty victories in battle was meant to teach the people to place their trust in divine power rather than in their own weapons. The memorable wars under Joshua and Gideon were fought from weakness rather than strength. Through several commands the Lord ordered Gideon to reduce his forces from thirty-two thousand to three hundred "lest Israel vaunt themselves against me saying 'My own hand has delivered me' " (Judges 7:2). The troops simply marched, blew their trumpets, smashed their jars, held their torches and cried, "A sword for the Lord and for Gideon!" and their enemies fled. If read carefully these stories offer little support for the peace through strength mood of a nation which places its trust in nuclear bombs instead of God. Nevertheless, such an interpretation is not entirely comforting to pacifists who find it difficult to reconcile a warrior God with the picture of God we have in Jesus Christ.

Both pacifists and nonpacifists might be helped by those who advise us to understand these stories in their own setting and learn the lessons God had for then and now. We need not regard them as the final model for our day. It is somewhat comforting to realize that other Christians have struggled with difficult issues. For example, it might help all of us to interpret such biblical texts, if we understood how some Christians can reject polygamy, capital punishment for adultery, the Saturday Sabbaths and Jewish ceremonial laws when all of these are sanctioned in the Old Testament.

The folk of the peace church tradition may make it too simple. When confronted with a text such as Leviticus 10:9 where God, through Moses, commands "every one who curses his father and mother" to be put to death, most would simply reply: "But that's not the way of Jesus." The most common hermeneu-

tic (principle of interpretation) of the peace churches has been
that the Old Testament must be interpreted in the light of the
New and both the Old and the New by the mind of Christ.

Redemption of All Peoples—God's Promise. The message
of the Old Testament is not limited to the narratives of the
redemption of God's people. In the beginning of the story (Genesis 12:1) God's blessing of Abram includes the promise that
through his nation all the families of the earth will be blessed.
The people were often reminded that they were once sojourners;
therefore, they should be hospitable and kind to sojourners and
strangers. This universal concern for all peoples was a part of
the message of the books of Ruth, Jonah and some of the
prophets. The punch line in the story of Jonah comes at the end
when God admonishes Jonah for being angry because the plant
which had provided shade for him had withered. If Jonah was
that much concerned about a plant which he did not make grow,
how much more does God pity the great city of Nineveh, in
which there are a hundred and twenty thousand children.

Such teachings are consistent with Isaiah's and Micah's
vision of the fulfillment of the promise to Abraham. The peoples
"shall beat their swords into plowshares, and their spears into
pruning hooks; nation shall not lift up sword against nation,
neither shall they learn war any more" (Micah 4:3). "The wolf
shall dwell with the lamb, and the leopard shall lie down with
the kid, and the calf and the lion and the fatling together, and a
little child shall lead them" (Isa. 11:6).

Some of the prophets began to proclaim that God's peaceable kingdom would come in other ways than through conquest.
It would come through a Suffering Servant. Whether or not one
believes that the suffering servant passages of Isaiah were
describing Israel's suffering or pointing to the coming Messiah
who would deliver the people, the New Testament writers
believed these texts described beautifully the ministry of our
Lord. The peace churches have felt justified in following the lead
of the gospel writers who, in interpreting the Way of Christ,
used these texts more than others.

Redemption—Shalom. Overshadowing the holy war stories, however, is the basic Hebraic understanding of peace. *Shalom* is the wonderful contribution of the Old Testament to the way of peacemaking. It is the same word as the word for salvation or redemption. For *Shalom* implies right relationship with both God and others. This Hebrew word is rich in content, pointing to integrity, community, harmony, wholeness, social righteousness and justice. Such is expressed in Psalm 85 where we discover that *shalom* is present where "mercy and truth are met together; righteousness and peace have kissed each other."

New Testament expressions of *shalom* depict what life in the new age is like. Jesus leaves peace with his disciples (Jn. 14:27). The preaching of the apostles is summarized in Acts 10:36: "You know the word which he sent to Israel, preaching good news of peace by Jesus Christ (he is Lord of all). Paul declares that Jesus "is our peace, who has made us both one, and has broken down the dividing wall of hostility" (Eph. 2:14). And we are to shoe our feet "with the equipment of the gospel of peace . . ." (Eph. 6:15).

Contrary to this biblical usage, Christians often have separated salvation from peace. Or they have failed to see the interrelationship between peace with God and peace with others. They have asserted that the church should stick to its business of saving souls. According to this view the church has no business in the arena of politics, dealing with questions of justice and peace. I agree with their assumption and differ with their conclusion. The church must be in the business of saving souls. In the Bible, however, the soul is a person, a whole person. To be engaged in the business of saving souls is to be involved in areas which bring people into better relationships with one another, with their creator and with creation. Salvation is a big business, including in the words of John Wesley, both individual and social salvation.

Scholars have accused Christianity of being just another mystery cult, similar to many other rival cults at the time of the appearances of the first Christian communities. The mystery religions primarily were involved in saving souls from this sinful world for immortality. An example is the cult of Mithra. An initiate was placed in a large pit. Cult members led a bull over the pit and slit his belly. The person was actually washed by blood. Through this washing the person was declared to have put on immortality. When it has been claimed that the early Christians constituted but another such salvation cult, most of us have objected. Christianity is concerned with personal salvation, but never in such a way which denies or escapes this world. With Judaism, Christianity retains the basic Old Testament concern for historical redemption, the desire that God's rule be manifest in the kingdoms of this world.

The golden text of the Bible for those who stress personal salvation is John 3:16. This beloved message offers the good news that God sent Jesus so that individual believers may know eternal life, a reality which according to the apostle, begins now. It is interesting to note, however, that John 3:16 is smack up against John 3:17: "For God sent his son into the world not to condemn the world, but that through him the world might be saved." Here one finds the golden text for personal religion right next a text stating God's intention to redeem the world.

Both being consistent with the biblical idea of *shalom*, these texts belong together. If you take John 3:16 without John 3:17, you can translate Christianity as a mystery cult only interested in saving souls from this sinful world to heaven. If you take the last verse without the first, Christianity becomes just another social movement lacking the power coming from deep personal commitment. We do need personally to accept Jesus Christ as Saviour and Lord. But this does not mean we are committed to a Saviour who calls us to be alone with him in the garden. Instead, we are disciples of One who calls us to be a part of his saving activity in the world.

The Way—Ethics

Imitation of the Way of the Cross. All three historic peace churches have emphasized dicipleship, literally meaning "following Jesus." This does not imply a rejection of his divinity. It

is because of his divine nature that his teachings and commandments have authority. He is both Saviour and Lord. Peace church
folk are drawn to texts such as this favorite: "He who says he
abides in him ought to walk in the same way in which he
walked" (1 Jn. 2:6).

This fundamental theme has led some to feel that the peace
church tradition is permeated with "Jesusolatry." Such worship
of Jesus can lead to a sentimental, personal attachment to a
"sweet" Jesus which neglects the offensiveness of his life style
and demands. An exclusive emphasis on an individual relationship to Jesus can also work against the acceptance of the risen
Christ as he comes through his body, the people of God. Biblical
scholars in the twentieth century have seriously criticized the
type of search for the Jesus of history in which we dress Jesus up
in our clothes or project our own image of an ideal on him and
worship that. In peace church circles Jesus may be presented too
often as a mild, peaceful rural character who loved everyone and
avoided all conflict.

If we ever feel we model completely the pattern of Jesus, we
can quickly fall into the sin of self-righteousness. Christ as
example becomes Christ as judge. His Way shows us up for who
we really are. This recognition brings us to our knees. We realize our need for grace. We imitate Christ and heed his leading
not because it is drilled into us to do so, but because he loves us
and because his love comes to us through the lives of others. The
reformation emphasis on God's forgiveness when we fail to be
disciples is a needed corrective to the Peace church emphasis on
the call to discipleship.[6]

Dietrich Bonhoeffer in his *Ethics* writes about conforma-
tion. Instead of stressing our efforts to be like Jesus, he focuses
on our need to allow Christ to take form in us. This may be yet
another way to combine the reformation themes of grace and
faith with the radical call for discipleship.

> This is not achieved by dint of efforts "to become like Jesus,"
> which is the way in which we usually interpret it. It is
> achieved only when the form of Jesus Christ itself works upon
> us in such a manner that it molds our form in its own likeness
> (Gal. 4:19).[7]

But what specific application does the debate over following Jesus have to peacemaking. John Howard Yoder, Mennonite theologian, has demonstrated that the biblical writers do not advocate an imitation of Christ except at one fundamental point, his cross. The New Testament writers do not hold up a sentimental and romantic mimicking of his style of life. We are not called to go barefooted in a Franciscan style of preaching. There is no advice to eat exactly as he ate or to dress as he did (though my sons were once fond of their pin which read, "Jesus wore long hair"). The New Testament call to discipleship does not set forward requirements to become carpenters or to choose twelve disciples.

The writers of the epistles and the gospels do focus, however, on following Jesus in the way of the cross. Paul can speak of the life of the Christian and of his ministry as dying and rising with Christ. We are to "walk in love, as Christ loved us and gave himself up for us" (Eph. 5:2). Hebrews 12 describes Jesus as the author and finisher of the kind of faith which might lead to suffering and death for the faithful. A similar destiny is predicted by the author of 1 Peter: "Since therefore Christ suffered in the flesh, arm yourselves with the same thought" (4:1). The theme is elaborated most clearly in the gospels: "If any man would come after me, let him deny himself and take up his cross and follow me. For whoever would save his life will lose it; and whoever loses his life for my sake and the gospel's will save it" (Mk. 8:34-35). The prayer of the early church seemed to be that of Ignatius: "Permit me to be an imitator of the passion of Christ, my God."

The believer's cross is not, then, every kind of sickness, suffering or tension which we have to endure from day to day. It is not the personal struggle of a sensitive soul with sin. Rather, it is the price of nonconformity paid when a Christian represents to an unwilling world the way of the kingdom which is to come. It is any manifestation of God's way of meeting evil in the world, the way of suffering love. This way renounces violence and the approval of existing injustice. At the same time it rejects attempts to maintain purity through noninvolvement. This is the cross which is a stumbling block for Christians, including members of the peace churches, and sheer foolishness to most people in our society. Nevertheless, this is the way in which we are called to imitate Jesus. When taken up with our own strength, the cross is a heavy burden. When taken up through the grace and power of God, the cross ultimately leads to joy and victory.

The Sermon on the Mount.

Blessed are the peacemakers, for they shall be called the children of God (Matt. 5:9).

You have heard that it was said, "You shall love your neighbor and hate your enemy." But I say to you, Love your enemies and pray for those who persecute you, so that you may be sons of your Father who is in heaven: for he makes his sun rise on the evil and the good, and sends rain on the just and on the unjust. For if you love those who love you, what reward have you? Do not even the tax collectors do the same? And if you salute only your Brethren, what more are you doing than others? Do not even the Gentiles do the same? You, therefore, must be perfect, as your heavenly Father is perfect (Matt. 5:43-48).

The peace church tradition has esteemed the Sermon on the Mount and in varying degrees has held it up literally as the life style for Christians. It often functions as a "canon within the canon." Generally, however, it functions as a commentary on Paul's affirmation that the whole law is fulfilled in love. For example, in the above passage perfection is not defined as a pattern, a code of ethics, or a static condition. Rather, to be perfect is to have something of the dynamic, inclusive, impartial nature of God's love, a love which includes the just and unjust, the good and the evil. Since pacifists so often waver between trying to follow the Sermon on the Mount and regarding it as an impossible ideal, it might be instructive to look at other perspectives.

Futuristic Ethic. For many persons the Sermon on the Mount describes the way things will be when Jesus returns and establishes his kingdom on earth. This way of perfect love has not been given for this present sinful age. Rather, it is a description of the way it will be in the future. Today, Christians must go to war. When the kingdom comes, however, there will be loving relationships between all.

Interim Ethic. It was Albert Schweitzer, the great scholar, organist and missionary to Africa, who proposed that in Matthew 5-7 we have an interim ethic, an ethic for those between the times. Jesus and his first followers anticipated an imminent end of the world. These teachings were given to the disciples for behaviour in this very unusual situation. They were not for all time. Since their expectations did not materialize, an ethical position for the long pull in a more stable society must of necessity be different. Since our present society is not all that stable and faces possible extinction, increasing numbers wonder whether the interim ethic of our Lord might be for such a time as this?

Personal Ethic. Martin Luther believed that the Christlike ethic of the Sermon on the Mount should guide all personal relationships. To typical questions of draft board members, a Luther-like response would be that it is wrong to take up arms to defend oneself. The Way of the Sermon on the Mount applies to the spiritual realm. But there is another realm, the temporal, which is likewise established as a divine order by God. In this realm, ethics are derived from natural law and reason. God can operate with a sword through the temporal rulers. Unlike some Anabaptist versions which proposed one kingdom for Christians and another for the state, Luther called every Christian to live in both realms. As an individual Christian one must not take up arms, but as a soldier who is commanded to do so by the state, one must kill for the sake of the neighbor.

Class Ethic. In the discussion of vocational pacifism we saw that there is another possible dualism between different classes. In the Roman Catholic tradition, for example, the hands that are used to consecrate the sacred bread, the body of Christ, should not be stained by blood. For this reason Roman Catholics have been insistent that conscription laws exempt clergy.

Absolute Ethic Not to be Followed. From the influential thinking of Reinhold Niebuhr we can derive yet another attitude. Niebuhr granted that Jesus embodied the nonresistant stance presented in the Sermon on the Mount. Responsible Christians cannot follow this way, however, for to do so would be to fail to be relevant to the great social problems of our day. If we enter this struggle, compromise is necessary. But it is right to have the ideal way of the Sermon before us. The perfect way of agape love in the lives of Jesus and others can help Christians who are in the struggle choose the lesser of two evils.

Law Ethic. Many have followed a traditional Protestant interpretation that the Sermon on the Mount is a new law added to the law of the old covenant. The purpose of law, old and new, however, is not that it be followed. This is impossible as anyone knows from reading the Sermon on the Mount. Its purpose, then, is to let us know how miserably we fail in living up to it. This realization of our own weaknesses and sin will bring us to see the need for the gospel of forgiveness. The function of the Law, including the Sermon on the Mount, is to bring us to the gospel.

Ethic to Be Obeyed. The Sermon on the Mount does not conclude with Jesus saying, "Verily, I have told you these things so that you might fall on your knees and ask for repentance." Rather it concludes with the comment: "Every one who hears these words of mine and does them will be like a wise man who built his house upon the rock; and the rain fell, and the floods came, and the winds blew and beat upon that house, but it did not fall, because it has been founded on the rock" (Matt. 7:24-

25). Dietrich Bonhoeffer echoes this conclusion in his commentary of the Sermon on the Mount:

> Humanly speaking, we could understand and interpret the Sermon on the Mount in a thousand different ways. Jesus knows only one possibility: simple surrender and obedience, not interpreting it or applying it, but doing and obeying it. That is the only way to hear his word. But again he does not mean that it is to be discussed as an ideal, he really means us to get on with it.[8]

We fail to find in the Sermon a list of entrance requirements into the kingdom. Rather, as a result of repentance, life is restructured in response to the kingdom. The Sermon is a part of the good news and not merely Law to prepare us for the gospel. It represents the style of God's coming realm in contrast to the present. The Beatitudes begin and end with the promise of the kingdom. The righteousness they proclaim is integrity before God and right relationships with one another. Pacifism, peacemaking, should not become law; it should rather represent a joyful response to and participation in the kingdom coming.

Love of Neighbor

And he said to him, "You shall love the Lord your God with all your heart, and with all your soul, and with all your mind. This is the great and first commandment. And a second is like it, You shall love your neighbor as yourself. On these two commandments depend all the law and the prophets" (Matt. 22:37-40).

Often, our obedience to the commandments has been far from a joyful response to the gospel of God's love. Rather it has been an effort to get to heaven. One good corrective is to focus on the second commandment. Loving our neighbor requires us to place persons above principles. The parable of the good Samaritan answers the question who is my neighbor by pointing to the deed of the Samaritan. The enemy becomes the neighbor through an act of love.

Hans-Werner Bartsch, visiting German New Testament scholar, in a series of lectures at Bethany Theological Seminary presented the commandment, love of neighbor, as the basis of New Testament personal and social ethics. Even Paul's advice to be "subject to the governing authorities" in Romans 13 stands between two love passages. The state, Bartsch maintained, has divine sanction only insofar as it helps us to love our neighbors. When it leads to the destruction of our neighbors, it loses its authority in some areas. We are required only to give obedience to whom obedience is due.

Professor Bartsch also reminded us that in the New Testament we have a reversal of the usual definition of neighbor. Ordinarily, our neighbors are those who live near us or those with whom we associate from day to day. If they were threatened, we would defend them to the last one. But the message of the New Testament says our enemy is our neighbor. The Chinese, the Russians, and the Africans are our neighbors as well as those who live nearby. Such an understanding makes blasphemy out of the usual assumptions behind military operations, namely, that an American life is worth more than the life of a citizen of another nation.

Bartsch added substance to the Anabaptist peace witness. He challenged us to regard the way of love as witness rather than obedience. Christian witness is a response to the deed of God's love. Witness implies that we are sharing and pointing to that which we do not possess but which by grace we have received. The test of whether or not we go to war must be a test of Christian witness. Can we proclaim the gospel to enemies by killing them?

Luther justified killing in warfare by saying that we are called to show love for our neighbors by protecting them from our enemies. Bartsch answered that when we say we kill for the sake of another in reality we may be justifying our murder by shifting the responsibility. It may be true that there are honorable reasons for participating in war, but murdering for the sake of the neighbor should not be understood as Christian love. According to Bartsch, "Christian love could not do anything wrong for the beloved either.'"[9] In concluding his case for Christian pacifism, he argued that unless and until participation in war can be seen as a witness to the presence of the kingdom, Christians should refuse to justify war.

Among many other biblical texts and themes, there is one more that is crucial—the message of hope. In the face of despair both inside and outside peace circles, there is an urgent need for fresh ways of speaking of hope.

5

Hope and the Nuclear Crisis

Einstein's oft-repeated prophecy remains all too true: "When we released the energy from the atom, everything changed except our way of thinking. Because of that we drift towards unparalleled disaster." Have we learned to live comfortably with the bomb? Is it a sin to build a nuclear weapon? How should Christians respond to the nuclear crisis? This chapter will not deal in detail with arms limitations talks, the nuclear freeze movements, or data concerning the alarming escalation of the nuclear arms race. Thorough analyses of these issues are available from trusted authors who are rooted in the life of the church.[1] Here it is intended to bring the peace church perspective into dialogue with varying responses to the nuclear crisis.

I sat with a deeply concerned group of Japanese at the International Friendship Center in Hiroshima. Following a period of sharing about the American peace movement, the conversation drifted to the discussion of the bomb. One of the survivors talked of her bitterness. Others quickly protested her wholesale condemnation of America; it was Japanese militarism, they contended, that was ultimately responsible for this horrendous event. In the midst of the debate an elderly man spoke quietly and lovingly. "It is time," he said, "to stop blaming, to forgive. What is needed is the resolve to make certain that it never happens again anywhere in the world."

But the beautiful spirit of forgiveness I frequently encountered in Japan has not been joined by a spirit of repentance in America. The vast majority of Americans believe it was right and necessary to drop the bombs in order to save American lives, this in spite of the growing body of historical evidence to the contrary. At a fortieth anniversary celebration of the explosion of the first bomb in New Mexico, one of the leading members of the Los Alamos team stated: "In junior high I read about how they built the bomb. I thought those people were wonderful. But it never occurred to me that I would be doing it. I think it's neat."[2] In 1959 Karl Barth, a Protestant theologian known for his bold witness against Nazism, declared that the most vital issue facing Christianity is the inability of the church to take a definite stand against nuclear weapons. Though there is growing concern within the churches, his statement, unfortunately, still applies to most of Christendom.

Invited to a community to share with churches and various peace groups, I was smuggled into a youth class by parents. The atmosphere was permeated with a spirit of indifference to me and any nuclear concerns. After unsuccessful efforts to establish contact, I stopped and emotionally shouted: "I am deeply concerned about these issues. It is obvious this is not your thing. Why isn't my thing your thing?" Having their attention, I waited. Finally, a sharp youth responded: "My mother and people like you run around to peace meetings, but it's not going to do any good. We are going to have a nuclear war. There is nothing we can do about it. Since we will not live as long as you have, we want to enjoy ourselves while we can."

Similar desires for instant gratification are found in popular religious expressions whereby Jesus saves us from the problems of the world and blesses us with health, success and prosperity. Many people are numb or complacent, or they refuse to acknowledge reality. They are satisfied and absorbed in busy routines. The tendency to hide from the truth has been advantageous to those who profit from these ghastly weapon systems. Some even reason: "God will not let it happen," a hope difficult to sell to the Japanese.

In times like these there may be no more important task than to interpret the meaning of Christian hope. We have been coping in various ways. But can we live at peace with the bomb? We must refuse to live out of despair. It is imperative that we proclaim in word and deed the good news of Christian hope.

Hope Without Compassion

Those who identify with premillenialism or various kinds of dispensationalism have taught me something about Christian realism, the truth that apart from God we cannot easily roll up our sleeves and build the kingdom of God on earth, the truth that things sometimes have to get worse before they can get better. It is reported that a popular singer talked enthusiastically about meeting Jesus in the skies at the time of the rapture. Just thinking about this event made his spine tingle. He became ecstatic dreaming of this journey even as he looked below and saw millions of people perishing in a nuclear holocaust.

In this kind of hope the rapture becomes the ultimate air raid shelter. It is hope without compassion. How different were the feelings of One who came to the Mount of Olives and looked over Jerusalem. Contemplating what might happen to that great city if its people did not change their ways, Jesus wept. His plea for them no doubt is his plea for us: "Would that even today you knew the things that make for peace" (Luke 19:41).

Jesus was pretty hard on some of the folk of his day who were working out schemes and looking for signs of the end. One of the times the Sadducees and Pharisees came to trap Jesus, they requested that he show them a sign from heaven. He spoke directly: It is "an evil and adulterous generation that seeks for a sign" (Matt. 16:4). Robert Jewett, Methodist New Testament scholar, suggests one reason Jesus may have been hard on people who were speculating about the end. They rejoiced in thinking of the salvation of a chosen few and the destruction of their enemies. Such hopes were self-serving and nourished a type of nationalism our Lord opposed. This mood was contrary to his commandments to be concerned about and to love all people.

Jesus added that no sign would be given except the sign of Jonah. Though this sign has been interpreted in a variety of ways, a fundamental message of that story was God's admonition to love even the wicked Ninevites. Jonah had sought to avoid preaching to those he despised, and he was angry when the city repented. The story of Jonah points to the power of the gospel to convert a wicked city. Could it be a sign that we can still believe in miracles? The sign of Jonah could be the crazy and wonderful hope that the Ninevehs of our day might defuse their horrible weapons.

Hope Without Freedom and Responsibility

I have also learned from the Bible and conservative Christians that the kingdom is God's and will come in God's time, not ours. Nevertheless, when history fails, when the arms race appears to be out of control, we desire to nail everything down. We want the details of our future existence spelled out neatly. When Jesus called the sign seekers adulterous, he might have been alluding to their unfaithfulness to the God of the open-ended future. Look at the many people today who are attracted to varieties of "pop" apocalypticism, sooth sayers and fortune tellers of all kinds. Those who chase after gods who can predict the future are unfaithful to the God who called Abraham "to go out to a place which he was to receive as an inheritance . . . not knowing where he was to go" (Heb. 11:8). We refuse to live by faith. We want to live by sight. We overlook passages of Scripture which assert that we cannot know the times or the seasons, and we ignore the Pauline admonitions that we can only know in part and our knowledge is imperfect.

The problem with hope based on a predetermined, detailed plan of history is that it lacks a place for human freedom and responsibility. Many Christians argue that because Jesus predicted there would be wars and rumors of wars, it is wrong for us to desire world peace. Efforts to eliminate war, therefore, are against God's will. Though this verse has been oft-quoted to pacifists, the prediction in the same passage concerning families facing persecution has been ignored. I have never met anyone who refers to the prophecy about a father putting his child to death and children rising up against their parents (Mk. 13:12) to argue against our striving for better family relationships.

However, this issue cannot be easily dismissed. It might be helpful to look at it in relation to the question of individual salvation. Historically, this question has been the essence of the debate between predestinarian Calvinists and free-will Arminians. Has God determined from the beginning that some part of the human race will go to heaven, do what they will, and the rest be damned do what they can? Sincere Christians will differ in their answers. In exploring the scriptures on this issue, I have been led to affirm both the providential working of God and human freedom. When I look back on certain events in my life, I can discern both the hand of God and my own free decision. We are only saved by the grace of God, but in wonderful ways God's grace works through and does not destroy human freedom. Many who reject absolute predestination in thinking of individual salvation, nevertheless, adopt a predestinarian analysis in thinking of the events of world history.

For the most part the peace church tradition has been within the Arminian tradition, affirming human freedom and responsibility. The thing we know about God more than anything else is that God is love. In creation we were created in the image of God. God has given us human freedom, placing responsibility in our hands. The nature of God's love is that it is not coercive. God will not force a divine plan on us. God's wrath is but the other side of God's love. This means that we are free to go to hell if we so choose. God's wrath would allow us to perish in a nuclear holocaust.

I do not believe we have any guaranteed promises in the Bible that God will prevent us from destroying this planet if we are so bent. It is difficult to imagine, however, that the God who gave the rainbow as a sign to Noah and visions of shalom to Isaiah wants war. Jesus could predict wars in light of the sinfulness of his time. But this did not mean that he favored wars as a part of God's plan. Neither did Jesus believe that war or a nuclear holocaust is inevitable. Why would he deny that persons could respond to his call to repent and receive the kingdom which was and is at hand. Whatever happens to this planet, faith, hope and love abide. Ultimately God's will and way will triumph and be vindicated. The whole wide world is in God's hands.

Hope Based on Realism
(Deterrence, Strength, Fear)

Reinhold Niebuhr has been mentioned because of his brilliant critique of pacifists. Those deeply influenced by his thinking have often been labeled critical realists, for they judge the pacifist approach to problems of peace and justice as naive; pacifists refuse to compromise and recognize the nature of entrenched evil. For many years I read *Christianity and Crisis*, a Niebuhrian periodical, in order to be in dialogue with those who most effectively critique pacifism. I still read it but find little with which to quarrel. The gap between critical realists and pacifists is narrowing.

Many critical realists have become nuclear pacifists. Contemplating nuclear war, they reason that the results would bring greater evil than the good which is defended. Even in examining more "conventional" wars, they find it difficult to identify conflicts which meet the just war requirements that innocents be protected and that violence will not escalate from concerns for defense to acts of vengenance and mass destruction.

In awe of critical realists, I refused for years to suggest that pacifism works. Instead I asserted that the case for pacifism rests on faithfulness to the Way of our Lord, trusting that this Way would participate ultimately in the kingdom coming. Now, I am beginning to sense with others that the scandal of the Jesus Way is becoming the only realistic alternative. What would realism dictate for places such as Poland? It is difficult to speak for them or for people in similar circumstances. Many sense that to do nothing would be wrong. To resist violently would elicit cruel repression. To call in the armaments of a superpower would invite the destruction of the culture and land. Increasing numbers of people find it better to use nonviolent forms of resistance or to accept suffering within the changing historical process than to risk or participate in mutual annihilation.

Likewise, it increasingly becomes obvious, that not all of the naive utopianism is to be found in the camp of the pacifists. When I have listened to just war analysts who make the case for possible limited nuclear exchanges, I agree with Stanley Hauerwas: "The possibility of a society sustaining the moral ethos necessary to support such a war seems as unlikely and utopian as a nation taking a pacifist stance."[3] Those participating in the escalation of the nuclear arms race refuse to heed the warning of scientists that unless the nuclear arms race is controlled, the odds will increase that the end of history will result from some chance occurrence instead of human decisions. Still, as Dale Aukerman writes, "The nuclear gamblers stay at the nuclear tables."[4]

Deterrence. Realists have viewed deterrence as a logical policy. The world has many trouble spots and many aggressive, totalitarian nations. Great arsenals, even including unthinkable weapons, deter aggressors and tyrants from doing what they might otherwise do. For nearly a half a century we have survived a nuclear stalemate. Neither superpower dares drop a bomb for fear of setting in motion missiles from the adversary. Such a balance of terror has been comfortably accepted by many because the worst fears have not been realized. The policy remains offensive to others because of the ghastly nature of the weapons, narrow escapes from catastrophe on several occasions, astronomical costs which rob the poor of their share of the world's resources, and the proliferation of such weapons when we already have enough of them to destroy everything in the world many times.

As I write there are many Americans, including Quakers, Mennonites and Brethren, who are not yet aware of a fundamental shift in policy. Replacing the policy of deterrence which has been dubbed MAD, mutually assured destruction, a new nuclear weapon's strategy has been properly named INSANE, instant strike anticipating nuclear exchange. It involves a counterforce strategy whereby MX, multiple warhead, and Trident missiles are targeted toward weapons instead of cities. The destabilizing nature of this change comes from the attempt to perfect the accuracy of weapons to the extent that it might be possible to knock out nearly all of the weapons on the other side and thereby eliminate the possibility of large scale retaliation. In case of a showdown between the two superpowers in some part of the world, one side might be tempted to begin such an exchange in fear that the other side might do so first. An additional destabilizing development emerges when such accurate missiles are placed in Western Europe and on submarines. Only a few minutes away from their targets, there will not be time for human decisions. This increases the chances of an accidental exchange due to a malfunctioning computer.

Such alarming developments makes most relevant a "peace and survival" report received from the section on deterrence of the World Council of Churches meeting in Vancouver in 1983. All old and new peace churches should be thankful for this statement which is commended to the churches for study and action:

> Nuclear deterrence is morally unacceptable because it relies on the credibility of the intention to use nuclear weapons: we believe that any intention to use weapons of mass destruction is an utterly inhuman violation of the mind and spirit of Christ which should be in us . . .

> Nuclear deterrence . . . is the antithesis of an ultimate faith in that love which casts out fear. It escalates the arms race in a vain pursuit of stability. It ignores the economic, social and psychological dimensions of security, and frustrates justice by maintaining the status quo in world politics. . . . It is the contradiction of disarmament because it exalts the threat of force, rationalizes the development of new weapons of mass destruction, and acts as a spur to nuclear proliferation by persistently breaking the "good faith" pledge of disarmament in the Non-Proliferation Treaty, thus tempting other governments to become nuclear-weapon states.[5]

Peace Through Strength. The reliance on deterrence has been part of the peace through strength philosophy popularized by those calling themselves the Moral Majority. Those who support the nuclear freeze movement and disarmament do so at least in part out of fear of the consequences of continual escalation. And those who advocate peace through strength do so in part out of great fear of communism. As those in the peace movement often gloss over the threat of the Soviet Union, so those in the moral majority exaggerate it. It is possible that the charge of a lack of realism has rightly been applied to both groups.

It often seems that mass paranoia propels the arms race. I encountered this in a trip to the Soviet Union as a member of a delegation hosted by the Russian Orthodox Church. As I listened to priests, peasants, and people on the streets, their great fear of America came through. They had vivid memories of losing over twenty million of their own people in World War II (60 times the loss of Americans). This accounted for their extreme fear of "nukes" in West Germany. Other visitors have heard the people express genuine fondness for the American people. But they fear greatly the policies of the American government which escalates the arms race and maintains bases around the globe in an attempt to control the world.

After returning from the Soviet Union, I found myself attending a peace seminar on Capitol Hill. At the State Department, the Pentagon, and Congress, the atmosphere was saturated with the same kind of paranoia. There was a tremendous fear of the Russians. In the Pentagon, a general briefed us with graphs and statistics to demonstrate how far behind the Soviet Union we were at that time. Later while discussing another topic the general exclaimed: "It's time to get tough with the Russians." I scratched my head and wondered out loud: "I really can't understand. If we are as far behind the Soviets in armaments as you have told us, it seems it would be most stupid to get tough with the Russians. If they are as bad as you say, it may be treason to keep telling them how far behind them we are; for they would surely take advantage of us." The general immediately waxed eloquent in giving us another set of statistics which showed that in many areas we are far, far ahead. He concluded: "You are in safe hands with the American military." All of this increased my conviction that it is indeed unrealistic, even utopian, to accept uncritically the rationale of big bureaucracies for getting bigger.

As suggested in the World Council of Churches statement, a peace through strength philosophy based on paranoia is truly the opposite of biblical faith in that love which casts out fear. Peace through strength proponents argue from fear and ignore the golden rule. If the Soviets were to say, "We know the only thing you understand is strength. Now, we are stronger so shape up," how would we respond? The answer is obvious. We would make ourselves stronger. This philosophy feeds the development of more and better weapon systems on both sides.

Moreover, it overlooks the truth that when two peoples are in a clinch of hatred, they become more and more alike. If our adversary denies human rights, we become like them in supporting regimes that deny human rights. The most basic fault, however, with peace through strength thinking is that it does little to change the basic problem. It completely ignores the ancient rabbinic teaching. The question to the rabbi was "Who is the mighty one?" The answer was Jesus-like: "The one who converts his enemy into his friend." Exchanges and dialogue with our enemies help to reduce paranoia and increase trust.

Dare we trust the Soviets? Dale Aukerman compares our plight with a patient who is advised to have open heart surgery. He is practically certain to die without it but has a twenty per cent chance to live by submitting to the operation. It may be risky to trust the Soviets enough to take concrete steps toward disarmament. But it is even more risky to continue the arms race. William Sloane Coffin points out that we do trust the Soviets when it is to our advantage to sell them grain. We do not have to like them or even trust them very much, he says, to believe that they do not want to perish in a nuclear holocaust any more than we do. Christians need to take the risk of faith and love in times when fear motivates people to contemplate Satanic deeds.

Hope Based on the Will to Survive
(Fear of Mutual Suicide)

Physicians for social Responsibility offer a medical analogy. A dying patient refuses to take the necessary steps to prevent death and fantasizes that she can survive whatever may come. All plans and preparations for surviving a nuclear war are dangerous fantasy. Prevention is the only possible remedy.

Sidney Lens, veteran peace activist, was invited to speak at a luncheon meeting at a Church of the Brethren Annual Conference. He thundered like an Old Testament prophet delivering his doomsday predictions. If we continue in our present course, he warned, we are destined to perish. His call to repentance was heavy diet for many Brethren who had purchased luncheon tickets in the convention center in order to avoid the steamy heat of the streets. After he finished, I overheard a radical Christian talking to the speaker. "Sidney," he said, "preaching the doomsday message to them outside the context of the gospel message of hope will not do any good. They will walk out and deny, dismiss or repress what you said. You certainly will not motivate them by preaching this way." Sidney Lens responded immediately: "I did exactly what I intended. I wanted to scare the hell out of them so they will repent."

I have mused a lot about this exchange. We have had this issue around for a long time. We have had hell-fire preachers who could describe the temperature of hell so vividly that people responded to the altar call from fear. Early Methodist preachers were among those who called people "to flee from the wrath to come." Their leader, John Wesley, approved. yet he felt a corrective was needed. People will not get to heaven, he advised, because they are afraid they are going to hell. Ultimately, they only will make it to heaven if they are drawn by the love of God.

There is a lesson in this for the peace movement. We need to be realistic. It is right to show movies about what will happen if nuclear fuses are triggered. Our message must not offer escape from the worst scenarios of our era, but rather hope in the face of them. The call to wake up or blow up is an expression of the biblical call to repentance.

But the call to repentance must be given as part of the message of hope which keeps alive the great biblical visions of life as it should be lived on this planet. These visions dream of a world where swords will be beaten into ploughshares so justice will flow like a mighty stream. People can be motivated through fear, but often fear evokes ill-advised and reckless responses. A more permament peace will come when people are inspired by love, when they live out of the great visions of peace and justice. Christians should be people who know that "there is no fear in love, but perfect love casteth out fear" (1 Jn. 4:18).

However, pacifists are not strict survivalists. Life is sacred because of God's intention in creation. But life is not an end in itself. There are things for which we should be willing to die because of One who is greater than life itself. We would rather be dead than unfaithful to our Lord. This does not mean we can join those who claim they would rather be dead than red if that means annihilating millions of Soviet citizens including our own brothers and sisters in Christ.

As we can critique the collective self-righteousness of many who exalt Americanism as a moral end to be defended at all costs, we can also question the philosophy which holds human survival to be the ultimate good. The position of survivalists and nuclear pacifists is based largely on responses to the nuclear threat rather than on a desire to understand the nature of Christian witness.

In spite of these differences, we rejoice in the growing numbers of nuclear and survivalist pacifists. We share their fervent desire to avoid a nuclear holocaust. We discern biblical concerns in their love for God's creation. We applaud their boldness in telling it like it is with our doomsday plans and telling it like it will be if we ever have a nuclear exchange. All who long for peace, and we hope that includes all followers of the Prince of Peace, should join hands with the survivalists. In raising the consciousness of all with the apocalyptic message of doom, let us permeate this growing awareness with an apocalypticism of hope.

The Nature of Resurrection or Apocalyptic Hope

It was a bit surprising to encounter one of the most dramatic expressions of the apocalyptic in the pages of the *New Yorker*. In prophecies in his book, *The Fate of the Earth*, Jonathan Schell graphically described how the use of nuclear weapons would mean the destruction of the human species.[6] Apocalyptic is another word for revelation or unveiling. Schell dramatically unveiled scenarios of the end of life as we know it on our planet. If he is taken seriously at all, we can discern close relationships between our era and that of the period before and after the birth of Jesus.

Then, the Jewish people lived under the threat of the extinction of their nation. Today, we live under the threat of the destruction of our civilization from nuclear weapons. Both eras may be characterized by a pervading sense of despair following earlier periods of optimism. These similarities, no doubt, have contributed to the current revival of interest among biblical scholars in apocalyptic literature.

These ancient writings emerged during the period between the Testaments. Most of them were not accepted as a part of our canon. An exception is the book of Daniel which was written when Antiochus IV Epiphanes (175-163 b.c.) tried to exterminate the Jewish religion. The last book of the Bible was penned from prison to encourage people facing persecution. It is named the Apocalypse or Revelation of John. Prophetic literature had kept hope in the future alive by telling the story of God's faithfulness to Israel in the past. Apocalyptic writers used pictorial images and cosmic visions to inspire hope in spite of historical evidence and trends to the contrary.

For years New Testament scholars regarded this literature as less than Christian. It seemed to be contrary to the spirit of Jesus to rejoice in the destruction of our enemies. More recently, however, scholars have realized that apocalyptic themes are the foundation for much of New Testament thought. For example, the first beatitude may be the combination of a wisdom saying, "Blessed are the poor in spirit," with an apocalyptic promise about the kingdom. Pauline death and resurrection themes are apocalyptic expectations of life and hope in the midst of death and despair.

The Future Breaking into the Present. Whereas many expressions of the apocalyptic seem to be limited to doomsday prophecies, biblical apocalypticism combines a pessimistic reading of history with an optimistic hope in God's redemption. Contrary to many popular interpretations which assign the kingdom entirely to the future, biblical hope is possible because the future kingdom breaks into the present. Hope does not come from a backward look. Christians are motivated because they see the future kingdom breaking into the present as a powerful force. As Quakers have stated it, God's light, the living Christ is still at work in this thick night of darkness.

The Now, but Not Yet Nature of the Kingdom. Eternal life may have been John's version of the kingdom theme of other gospel writers. His message proclaimed hope in eternal life after death. Yet eternal life begins now. This way of thinking of individual salvation may be applied to historical redemption. The kingdom of peace and righteousness will come in fullness only in the future. Yet Jesus proclaimed that the kingdom is at hand.

As a boy I was mystified by one statement of the Brethren at love feast time. They referred to the agape meal we ate together as a Messianic banquet and looked forward to that day when our heads would be resting on Abraham's bosom. After a long time I think I have finally come to some understanding. As we sit around the tables which symbolize our love for one another, we know that we are far from knowing the perfect love for one another and for Christ which God desires. Nevertheless, we can experience a foretaste of the community which God desires for all people. We can eat the first fruits of the victory banquet which will take place when the Messianic reign comes in fullness.

Though the kingdom is not yet, we can point to and participate in signs of its coming by preaching good news to the poor, proclaiming release to captives and setting free those who are oppressed (Lk. 4:18). Whenever we join in the things that make for peace and justice, we participate now in the coming kingdom at the same time realizing that the perfect kingdom continues to transcend and judge our imperfect understandings and feeble efforts. When we pray, "Thy kingdom come." we acknowledge both the now and not yet nature of the kingdom.

Hoping for surprises. The biblical apocalyptic expresses hope in spite of the way the world is going, hope which holds fast to the promises of God in spite of the failure of history. This message keeps alive hope in the coming of the new in the face of contrary evidence. Biblical hope does not advise us to run away from dismal facts. It does call us to look at the facts in light of the promises of God.

In meeting with political science classes on a college campus, I was intrigued to discover this same teaching reflected in the writings of a political philosopher. Hannah Arendt chides historians for basing their predictions about the future entirely on what they know about the past and present. She maintains that to call events which are not expected, "random events," is the oldest trick in the trade to lull us to sleep. For the possibilities of the unexpected far exceeds the wisdom of scholars.[7] Apocalyptic hope remains open to something new entering history. Resurrection hope implies possibilities of the unexpected. We should pray for, live and act as though we really do believe in surprises. This point is echoed by Jim Wallis when he asserts that the only people who belong in the peace movement are those who believe in miracles.

As one who has been in the peace movement over thirty years, I testify to the presence of apocalyptic hope. If my motivation had depended on success in stopping the arms race, I would have become a burned out disillusioned "peacenik" long ago. There remains hope in spite of all our failures. There are signs that a powerful new advent of biblical shalom may be possible.

Shortly before his death, I had an inspiring visit with Harold Row, architect of Brethren and Church World Service projects. He told me spiritually that he was ready to die. At the same time he talked of possible new cures and dreamed of how he would serve in the future. I have come to see the logic in this contradiction. As Christians, we should live courageously and prophetically in the face of possible annihilation. At the same time we need to live and plan as if our world will continue for a long time. Ours is an apocalyptic hope, a hope which refuses to be buried in evidence pointing to a nuclear holocaust, a hope that something radically new can break into our present history. This hope requires concrete expressions in peacemaking. This hope asks us to watch and pray though we know neither the day nor the hour when the kingdoms of this world will become the kingdom of our Lord.

I have shared the story of Peter Ediger and a Mennonite congregation in Colorado many times. The story beautifully expresses the nature of apocalyptic hope. This little congregation marched around buildings at the nearby Air Force Academy. After the seventh time, they blew their little horns. Later when Peter was telling about this, someone interrupted him at the crucial spot: "But did the walls fall down?" To which Peter responded, "No, but they will." This is a dramatic sign of the witness of a little peace church against a powerful symbol of the military industrial complex. The walls did not collapse but arrangements were made for dialogue sessions between the Mennonites and students at the academy. It seems absolutely absurd to compare the pigmy witness of the motley little group with the power and influence of the Pentagon. Yet apocalyptic faith claims that the foolishness of the cross is wiser than the wisdom of the powers. Apocalyptic hope promises that the future is with the meek not with those who have the ability to dispense death from the skies. The walls will fall and we can begin to live in this reality. Listen to the apostle Paul:

> In my opinion whatever we may have to go through now is less than nothing compared with the magnificent future God has planned for us. The whole creation is on tiptoe to see the wonderful sight of the sons of God coming into their own. The world of creation cannot as yet see reality, not because it

chooses to be blind, but because in God's purpose it has been so limited—yet it has been given hope. And the hope is that in the end the whole of created life will be rescued from the tyranny of change and decay, and have its share in that magnificent liberty which can only belong to the children of God! . . . We were saved by this hope . . . (Rom. 8:18-21, J.B. Phillips trans.)

6

Peace, Justice, and Liberation

"Justice and peace have kissed." (Ps. 85:10)

A memorial resolution for Martin Luther King at the meeting of the World Council of Churches in Uppsala, Sweden, called for the assembly to promote studies on nonviolent methods of social change. Pacifists saw this as an opportunity to raise the consciousness of the Council concerning the things that make for peace. At the same time the help WCC gives to groups combatting racism stimulated a debate about the use of violence in struggles for social justice. After many consultations, including those with third world and peace church Christians, a document entitled, "Violence, Nonviolence, and the Struggle for Social Justice," was commended to the churches for study. The Central Committee of the WCC noted the new context for the discussion:

> While violence is by no means a novel problem for the Christian conscience, our perception of the problem is in some respects new. In earlier years, the discussion focused almost exclusively on the "just war" and whether, or under what conditions, the Church should sanction the use of violence by sovereign states. Then Christians were deeply concerned about the morality of their individual participation in warfare, or in particular wars. The present document sets the whole issue in the wider context of the struggle for social justice, as it affects both oppressors and oppressed.[1]

A pacifist friend of mine sighed and said: "We have won the debate with the just war people. In our kind of world you really have to stretch and bend the just war principles in order to come out any other way than a pacifist. Now the liberation theologians confront us with the hard issues related to structural violence. And we are forced to struggle anew with our position." How right she is. For years I felt that I lived nonviolently. I had never killed anyone and was nice to most people. It was in the civil rights movement of the sixties that my heart as well as my head began to recognize what has been called structural, systemic, or institutionalized violence. When three black children died in the bombing of a church in Birmingham, Alabama, we were reminded that proportionally there are more black than white children who also die in the same city each year from the lack of proper nutrition and health care. These deaths come from the way our institutions are organized. The victims are just as dead as if they had been stabbed, shot or burned. When large tracts of fertile land are used to produce coffee for North Americans instead of food for the hungry families of the workers who make five hundred dollars per year producing the coffee, this is structural violence. Such covert violence kills just as surely as overt violence. It is no longer adequate to talk only about acts of violence in the slums; we must also talk about the violence of having slums.

Though I am a pacifist I have become aware that my hands are not bloodless. In struggling to identify with the oppressed, I have realized that I belong to every category of the oppressors. I am a white, male, middle class North American. As one who participates in violent structures I pray for mercy, trusting that the God who is good enough to forgive me is powerful enough to change structures and me.

The Peace Churches and Revolutionaries

In defending the peace stance, peace church apologists have often played down their revolutionary origins. Peace traditions emerged from a milieu of intense social and political unrest. The demand for social and economic justice brought about the Peasants' War of 1525. An estimated 100,000 commoners were slaughtered by the troops of the nobles. During the same year a little group of defectors from Zwingli, the Swiss Brethren, established the first Anabaptist congregation. Though they concluded that the sword was outside the perfection of Christ, one of their leaders, Conrad Grebel, addressed the revolutionary Thomas

Muentzer as a brother in Christ. In seventeenth century England, the Quakers emerged as the nonviolent wing of a militant Puritan revolution, which included Muentzer-like Fifth Monarchists and Diggers.

Reformation scholar Lowell Zuck has documented the relationship between the violent and nonviolent wings of the radical reformation in a collection of free church documents, *Christianity and Revolution.* Though the separatist pacifist position was in some ways the polar opposite of Muentzer's violent revolution, both positions were equally offensive and illegitimate to the establishment of that day, including Luther and Calvin. The fact that the nonviolent rather than the violent communities survived and grew serves as an interesting historical footnote.

What they had in common was the discovery of a gospel that spoke to their economic hardships and social inequality. In the Bible, which had recently become available to the masses, they read of a God who led people out of political bondage in Egypt into the promised land. Their Jesus lived among the common people and had hard words for the wealthy and pretentious people of the day. He taught that all were brothers and sisters and should care for one another. Members of peace churches who claim continuity with the faith of their radical forbears live out of a heritage of ideas that are strikingly similar to basic themes of liberation theology.

The historical experience of the peace churches has been that "God chose what is low and despised . . . what is weak in the world to shame the strong" (1 Cor. 1:27). At its best, therefore, the peace church tradition identifies with those at the bottom of social structures. Doing something for "the least of these" is applied to both those inside and outside of the community of faith. There is an egalitarianism exemplified by the role of women among the early Friends. Espousing an allegiance to Christ which supersedes all others, the peace churches often favor democratic more than hierarchical structures in family, church and government.

Jesus came to bring liberty to the captives, freedom to the oppressed, and good news to the poor. The peace churches have known a heritage leavened with justice concerns. Contemporary differences in expressing these concerns were there in the beginning. Whereas some radicals sought to achieve justice by influencing structures at the top, violently or nonviolently, others located the center of divine justice in the community and in the sharing of things in common. Both groups defined sin as social, the destruction of community whether in society or in the church. In present Christian liberation movements, right practice (*orthopraxis*) is as important, if not more important than right doctrine (*orthodoxy*). Doing justice as well as believing that one is justified marks a Christian.

Among contemporary movements that resemble the early peace churches are the hundreds of thousands of base Christian communities mushrooming in Latin America and in other parts of the world. Where people are too poor to pay professional clergy, women and men lay leaders emerge to become active servants of the word and the church. Members pray, encourage, support and admonish one another. In the spirit of solidarity the base communities are a counter movement to the society that oppresses them. Growing largely from Catholic soil, they mix ingredients of the Catholic Mass with old-fashioned prayer meetings, Methodist Bible classes, politicizing cadres, and penetecostal celebrations. They embody in one way or another, the hermeneutic (interpretation) of liberation theology, namely, the bias of the biblical writers for the oppressed. The Bible is a book of the poor, written by the poor for the poor. Resembling the pluralism of the Radical Reformation, some base communities support freedom fighters, others opt for nonviolent change, while still others are more apolitical.

The Place of Jesus
Those who support violent resistance argue that in many situations the choice is not between violence and nonviolence. Structural violence is so pervasive that they must choose between the lesser of two evils. To do nothing is to allow wretched conditions resulting in systematic death to continue. Nonviolent resistance often evokes cruel torture and repression

leaving no other option than violence. Many believe that less suffering results from revolutionary violence than from undisturbed misery and degradation.

Because the coming of Jesus was accompanied by revolutionary promises, violent resistance is viewed as a way to participate in the Messianic promise. The expectations found in the beautiful Song of Mary (Lk. 1:52-53) are heard gladly by many third world Christians:

> He has put down the might from their thrones, and exalted those of low degree; he has filled the hungry with good things, and the rich he has sent empty away.

Juan Pico of Nicaragua argues that Christ's humanity meant that his actions were limited by his circumstances. Even though Jesus himself did not take up arms, self-sacrificing deeds which lead to greater justice for the good of the total community are Christ-like actions.[3]

On the other hand, many base communities and some liberation theologians agree with the pacifist perspective of Dom Helder Camara, archbishop of Recife, Brazil. He offers his conclusions in a small book entitled *Spiral of Violence* (1971). He defines three kinds of violence: injustice, revolt, and repression. When structural violence or injustice becomes too repressive, revolt breaks out. In turn revolt invites even heavier-handed repression such as death squads. Violent responses lead to more violence and even greater suffering. And so the spiral continues. According to Camara, the demonic spiral can only be broken by the power of love. Realistically, nonviolent responses also entail much suffering, but they potentially offer more hope for ultimate reconciliation. Camara and other advocates of nonviolence do not speak as spectators. They are actively involved in the struggles of their people. Their Christ is one who liberates people from oppressive structures as well as sins. And such liberation implies the suffering love of a nonviolent cross.

The fact that the incarnation occurred in a revolutionary era is easily passed over in Bible study by North American Christians. But God sent the Son into a country seething with revolutionary activity and violence. Judas the Maccabee and his brothers, through bloody guerrilla warfare, had ushered in a century of Jewish freedom in the year 160 B.C. This freedom from foreign domination came to a bitter end in 63 B.C. when the Roman general Pompey desecrated the temple and the Sabbath in a bloody slaughter of 12,000 Jews. As a boy Jesus may have observed the suppression of an insurrection in a nearby village. God sent Jesus to a people eager to throw off the yoke of repressive foreign domination.

The Zealots were a party that came out of this revolutionary milieu. Many of their first names, the Simons, the Judases and the Johns, reveal their identification with the early Maccabean freedom fighters. Filled with nationalistic spirit and zeal for the Jewish law, they hoped to restore independence through violence. They were a people's party, hostile to the rich and sympathetic to the poor.

In this revolutionary atmosphere, where did Jesus belong? In the eyes of people in power at Jerusalem, Jesus was no doubt a Zealot. He was killed for treason. The charge written above his head accused him of attempting to be king of his own people. The popular support which greeted his entry into Jerusalem and his radical activity in the temple may have motivated the officials to take immediate action to avoid an uprising. It is known that there were Zealots among the twelve disciples. One was called "the Zealot," two were "sons of thunder" who desired to call down fire from the sky, and Peter, who cut off the soldier's ear, was far from a pacifist. Some have conjectured that as many as half of the twelve might have indentified in some way with these revolutionaries.

S. G. F. Brandon in a controversial book, *Jesus and the Zealots*, which was published in 1967, argues that Jesus was a near Zealot even if he did not belong to the party. Brandon believes that Mark wrote his gospel at the time Christians were threatened with persecution in Rome. Consequently the authors of the gospels began to make the case that Jesus was a mild pacifist who was killed at the hands of the Jews instead of a militant condemned by the Romans. Although the picture of Jesus given by New Testament authors makes Brandon's thesis questionable, it may be more plausible than the thesis that places Jesus solidly with the establishment. However, we also need to acknowledge that Jesus associated with tax collectors, even selecting one for his group of twelve.

Peace church exegetes insist that Jesus was nonviolent. He may have supported some of the goals of the Zealots but not their means. It is true that Jesus was much more than a political activist. It is wrong, however, to see him as one who dealt solely with spiritual and not social matters, with personal ethics and not concerns for peace and justice. Biblical scholars are rediscovering the political and revolutionary nature of his message.[4]

Bad Vibes from the Peace Churches

From the radical Episcopal theologian, John Pairman Brown, I first heard the expression "establishment pacifism," a phrase that showed me what many who struggle for justice and freedom must think of members of the peace churches. In the desire to be acceptable, we no longer identify with the oppressed. We have become cooperative citizens in the military industrial complex. Brown's judgment is severe: "Respectable pacifism is novocaine to deaden our awareness of complicity; it's the Establishment's ultimate technique for castrating our resistance."[5] Establishment pacifists identify more readily with the slogans and tactics of the wealthy and powerful than with the plight and causes of the poor and dispossessed. They join in naming the violence of the rich, "defense against communism," while labeling the violence of the poor, "terrorism."

"Cool It, Keep your Place." The year I taught as visiting theologian at Berea College, I offered a course on violence and nonviolence. In introducing the issues, I openly confessed my pacifism. Some students from Appalachia were scandalized to learn that someone might question the sacred notion that one always does what the nation requires. Among the students were blacks from American cities along with brothers and sisters of

freedom fighters in Latin America and Asia who reacted even more negatively. Here, a comfortable middle class American, a profiteer from his nation's oppression of others, was telling them to "cool it" in their struggles for greater justice.

This experience resembled an encounter in which conservative rural Brethren dialogued with black brothers and sisters from a large city. The conversation was lively and engaging. Sermon on the Mount passages such as turning the other cheek, going the extra mile, and praying for one's enemies were applied. Coming from those who have everything to those who struggle for equal rights, such teaching was patronizing and demeaning.

Such an approach needs a corrective. When Paul advised Christians to obey the law in order not to offend others, he argued that one could do so out of new found freedom in Christ. From the women's movement we learn that it is not Christian to be subject to others because it is required or expected. Rather, because one knows one's own freedom and dignity in Christ, one can lovingly and willingly be truly a person for others. In Christ there is neither Jew nor Greek, slave nor free, male nor female (Gal. 3:28). We can never support oppressive structures by teaching people to be subservient to them. The way of suffering love cannot be coerced. It is voluntarily given out of a faith which knows equality, dignity and freedom in Christ.

Pacifism as Passivism. Often pacifism does not mean making peace, which is the root meaning of the Latin word. Rather, pacifism means passivism. In our comfortable existence, we appear to be passively indifferent to injustice. The media and "junk" mail inform us of so many needs that our compassion lacks focus or quickly evaporates. Seduced by the false security of our armed might and high standard of living, we utter "peace, peace where there is no peace" (Jer. 6:14).

A Mennonite missionary wrote from Nicaragua when there was great fear of imminent invasion. More youth were being trained for war. In this atmosphere he tried to talk about nonresistance. A youth asked him directly: "What will the Mennonites in America do if your country invades Nicaragua?" He wrote that he was silent. He was reluctant to answer honestly. He feared that most American Mennonites would say or do nothing. Whether we like it or not, we are involved in a nation that is responsible for much violence and misery in the world. We need to trust our brothers and sisters in oppressed situations and our own members with firsthand experience to guide us in finding concrete ways to express our desire for justice and peace.

Band-Aid Strategies. It is not all that strange that the largest building in the Church of the Brethren is a mammouth warehouse at New Windsor, Maryland, which houses the offices of Church World Service. From there material goods can be dispensed quickly by truck and plane to needy areas around the world. The Mennonite Central Committee operates a multimillion dollar program of humanitarian and service ministries on behalf of several denominations. And the American Friends Service Committee continues to be a catalyst for peace education and a trusted agency for humanitarian concerns, attracting strong support from deeply concerned people outside the peace church tradition.

The fact that these ministries have often been so well-received by our society makes peace church members reluctant to protest the false priorities and injustices in our nation. More basic than this criticism, however, is the charge that these efforts represent a band-aid approach. We bind up wounds but fail to deal with basic causes. The peace churches focus on peacemaking and neglect the biblical mandates for justice. We have not learned, it is charged, that there is no peace without justice.

As a participant in a consciousness-raising seminar for North Americans in Cuernavaca, Mexico, I became deeply aware of this criticism. In one of the sessions the work of Mother Teresa, whose order serves in one of the worst slums of Calcutta, was cited as a supreme example of what Christians should not be doing. In her compassionate ministries, it was maintained, she is helping to soothe terrible conditions and thus delaying radical changes that are desperately needed.

In spite of my uneasiness, I felt those of us from the churches needed to hear what was being said. We defended alms-giving and ministries to basic human need as integral parts of the Judeo-Christian tradition. Then I thought about what happens in the peace churches. Those who put on the most band-aids are often the ones who desire the most to eliminate the source of the infection. Members who work with migrants quickly become involved in issues of social justice. Youth who lived with refugees in Central America preach justice when they come home. Relationships with individual prisoners lead to serious critiques of, and new models for, our criminal justice system. We are learning the truth of the advice of Pope John XXIII: "If you want peace, work for justice." And the long-held emphasis on simple living takes on new meaning as we see how our affluent life-styles contribute to gross injustices in the human family. Insofar as pacifists care about justice there they will be in contact with liberation movements. As we realize that there can be no peace without greater justice, we may also be called to witness to our historic message that there will be no lasting justice without peace.

Possible Contributions

Do pacifists have the right to speak of contributions of pacifism to theologies and movements of liberation? A visiting professor at Bethany Theological Seminary did not know he had a poor Brazilian student in one of his seminars. At one point in the discussion this student criticized liberation theologians who advocate the use of violence. The guest professor replied that it was easy to say this from "our" comfortable vantage point, removed from the struggles. Out of this awkward and embarrassing situation we might draw some conclusions. First, most North Americans are armchair theologians whether we advocate nonviolence *or* violence. Second, we speak more authentically if we are doing something about our concerns for justice. Third we should take the advice that the student from Brazil gave and offer our heritage of peacemaking without making so many apologies. Fourth, as members of a society producing horrendous weapons of death, we must repent and be humble. We must remove the beam of violence from our own eye before moralizing about the speck of violence in the eye of another.

Consciousness-Raising About the Superpowers. We can learn about ourselves from other peoples. They will challenge our basic assumptions. We can learn that it simply is not true that anyone who works hard can prosper and enjoy the "good" life. We can learn that our nation and corporations often bring bad rather than good news to many of the peoples of the world. At the same time we need to explain our situation to others, for we live under a different kind of oppression. Liberation theologians inform us that we cannot expect hungry people to have our great fear of a nuclear holocaust. We should remind people of President Eisenhower's statement: "Every gun that is made, every warship launched, every rocket fired signifies in the final sense a theft from those who hunger and are not fed, those who are cold and not clothed." The arms race of the superpowers is a vital link in the chain of oppression enslaving peoples around the world.

The small peoples of the world are victimized by the cold-hot war. An African proverb puts it well: "When two elephants fight, the grass suffers." Avoiding, so far, the self-destructive use of their nuclear arsenals on one another, the superpowers, nevertheless, become involved as adversaries in nearly every conflict situation in the world. Military assistance, advisors, covert aid, and even barbaric weapons such as napalm and anti-personnel bombs are provided. Tragically, it is the bodies of third world peoples, who for the most part are maimed and killed. Third world families, not Americans or Russians, are uprooted from their homes to become desperate refugees.

It was in this kind of talk about the relationship of the East-West conflict to North-South inequities that the third world students at Berea and I began to draw closer together. They sensed that my pacifist witness against the arms race was a vote for getting our feet off of their backs. Though not completely in agreement, they no longer felt that my most basic concern required them to "cool" their desire for justice. Rather they came to share my longing that third world bodies not be sacrificed as pawns in East-West power struggles.

Nationalism. The peace churches through their history have been pilgrim churches, relating to a wide variety of governments. We have needed to make it clear that our loyalty to our Lord is supreme and sets the limits for our lesser loyalties to the State. A logical conclusion of this faith has been that Christians should be committed to the good of all of the peoples of the world not just the national interests of their own land. Out of this background it is natural for peace churches to raise reservations about nationalism.

First, it would be foolish to say that peoples moving toward liberation should not nurture national identities to inspire their struggles. The sacrifices made to establish national identity need to be respected. However, new nations generally believe that the defense of their borders requires large military expenditures and the concentration of governmental power. This leads to the possibility that in the long run liberation movements may do little more than exchange one oppression for another. What the world desperately needs is not more nationalism, but less. Instead of supporting the proliferation of separate nations, the peace movement should keep alive the vision of a world in which nationalism will no longer divide people.

Repressive Violence. A Brazilian student, Onaldo Pereira, told us about the poorest of the poor. He stated that they truly do not feel deeply about the arms race. Neither do they always understand the speeches of the ideologically elite in the avant garde of guerrilla movements. All their efforts are focussed on securing enough to keep their children and themselves alive. Out of love for his people, Pereira favors the kind of *conscientization* (consciousness-raising) which motivates people to desire and work for greater justice.

However, Onaldo is also concerned about what happens when people are not informed of the risks of inviting the wrath and reprisals of the guardians of the status quo. He asks us to join him in calling the would-be liberator to prepare for the results of a kind of *conscientization* which fosters hatred. It can easily add to the burden of oppression and suffering already endured. In his country Onaldo reports that the rich live in a state of fear, building huge walls around their houses. Violent acts against them evoke the kind of rationalizations that lead them to justify death squads and barbaric forms of oppressive violence. In a world in which both left and right, liberation leaders and oppressive governments, often place ideology above the needs of people, it is right for Christians to speak on behalf of the rights and welfare of the people.

Witness Against Violence. Pacifists should beware of defending basic injustices or structural violence. It is difficult to dismiss lightly rebellion against structures that grossly violate God's people. Christians must remain true to their calling to decrease whatever violates the well-being of persons. At an international gathering of scholars, the question of systemic and counterviolence was being discussed. A case was being made for the latter whenever the former becomes extremely oppressive. A South African rose to his feet. His testimony was moving: "If the thing which is wrong with structural violence is violence, then the answer can never be more violence."

We learn from history that the violence that liberates can quickly become the violence that enslaves. When a new order of justice is created by murdering all who supported injustice, has injustice not merely changed hands! The way which is ultimately more revolutionary than violence is to repudiate the violent methods of your opponents. Pacifists who have demonstrated this most effectively include the martyrs who sealed the witness with their blood.

Witnessing Together for Justice and Peace
Even as I write there are events in the world which give me pause. I vacillate between feeling the contemporary relevance of pacifism and feeling the scandal and foolishness of proclaiming

the way of the cross. Whatever my moods, I am convinced that God calls us to preach Christ crucified. Although a stumbling block and foolishness to many, the cross is the power and wisdom of God. Whether or not others agree there are responses and interpretations we can share.

The Ministry of Listening. In our kind of world there are millions who are hurting, and many of them suffer because things are organized to our advantage. We are not sufficiently aware of oppressive structures. If we are informed, we often refuse to believe the reality of what we hear. Increasing numbers of Christians, through global contacts and personal relationships, have become aware of the deep pain and persecution of others. Many brothers and sisters from other countries come to us to share the hurts and stories of their peoples. This is a part of what is being called mission in reverse.

In our communities we have many opportunities to participate in the ministry of listening. When our own members are hurting, we want our pastor to give an ear. Yet we often refuse to do the same. It is difficult to pry Americans away from their TV sets and get them to listen firsthand as Christians from other countries share the deep suffering and repression of their people. It is painful to hear them express their anger over the policies of our nation.

Invitations to such meetings often have the feel of a political rally or social action meeting. In reality, the invitations summon us to engage in the ministry of listening. Christians should welcome the opportunity to bear another's burdens and thereby fulfill the law of Christ. So often we are immobilized by the magnitude of the barriers to peace and justice. Here is something visible and concrete that we can do. We can offer a compassionate and responsive ear to people who want to tell us the story of the suffering, persecution and oppression of God's people. In this way we can transcend our racist and nationalistic tendencies through fellowship with beautiful sisters and brothers in Christ.

Supporting Movements for Justice. It is often stated that violence becomes inevitable because nonviolent efforts are ignored or repressed. The efforts of Amnesty International have demonstrated how worldwide consciousness and prayer can make a difference in some cases, lessening torture and freeing political prisoners. Along with our concerns for countries embroiled in guerrilla wars with repressive regimes, Christians need to pay attention to nonviolent struggles largely ignored by the media. There are less volatile and publicized movements led by liberation theologians such as Dom Helder Camara and Adolfo Perez Esquivel.

Nobel peace prize winner in 1980, Esquivel has spent over a decade as an itinerant evangelist traveling from country to country in South America to coordinate and encourage nonviolent movements for justice. In and out of jail many times, Esquivel has met with peasants struggling against landowners in Ecuador, given support to the amnesty movement in Bolivia, helped create a Permanent Human Rights Assembly in Argentina, lent support to the National Peasant Union in Honduras and continues tirelessly to serve the cause of nonviolence and justice.

We need to make such ministries more visible, pray for them, and explore possibilities of mutual mission. It seems that such support is especially imperative for the peace churches. Many are zealously mobilizing public opinion against church programs which seem to sanction the use of violence in liberation struggles. Should not the peace churches join others in challenging these same voices to support as vigorously movements for justice which are nonviolent, Christ-centered and rooted in base Christian communities.

Laying Our Own Lives on the Line. Third world brothers and sisters often tell us that they cannot afford the pacifism of the American peace churches. Unlike us, they are not protected by naval fleets, marines, and the bill of rights. In their country this same military presence protects repressive governments that deny basic human rights. Consequently, they say our peace witness lacks relevance for their situation.

If we are convinced that Christ calls us to release the captives and to set at liberty those who are oppressed, we will be challenged to find nonviolent actions and reconciling programs. "In Christ's name we will continue to seek ways to prevent the violence of injustice, starvation, disease, and murder from taking place and will respond with loving concern after it has taken place. For it is not the radical following of Christ which holds us back from action, but rather the temptation of ease and conformity and the comforting half truth that our kingdom is not really of this world anyway."[6]

There are and will continue to be many opportunities to put our lives on the line. We can protest or resist paying taxes for violence. The Mennonite Central Committee is contemplating training people who would provide a nonviolent Christian presence in trouble spots where the presence of unarmed, praying Christians might help diffuse violent situations. At this writing a model of this is found in the Witness for Peace in Nicaragua. We can take the risk of declaring sanctuary or opening our churches and homes to refugees from injustice. These and other actions say, "In Christ's name we do not consent to this violence and place ourselves here as ones who are prepared to take the consequences."

Miguel d'Escoto is a Nicaraguan Christian and governmental leader who has pictures of Gandhi and Martin Luther King in his living quarters. Reflecting on Nicaragua's violent revolution, he notes that nonviolence was never a part of the teaching in the evangelization of Nicaragua. It was not until the people began to fight for greater justice that they were told it was wrong for them to use violence. His conclusion from this is simple and should go directly to our pacifist hearts: "We have no right to hope to harvest what we have not sown." Mennonite scholar C. Arnold Snyder, who quotes d'Escoto in his excellent lecture made into a pamphlet, offers sobering yet Spirit-filled responses. His challenge to Christians, especially those who wear the pacifist label, offers a fitting conclusion to this chapter.

If there is a [peace church] vision that we should recover for the future, surely it is the totally-engaged [discipleship] which dies to self only to rise fearlessly in Christ. Such discipleship will not shrink from acting on behalf of the powerless and violated, as we know Christ himself did when he was among us. God grant us the conviction to search together for the truth in all sincerity, and then the strength and courage to follow our Lord in life and deed.[7]

7

Disarming the Powers and Principalities

Invited to a large diocesan conference on peacemaking, I was surprised that they wanted an interpretation of Christian patriotism. I learned that Roman Catholics, long an ethnic minority in a Protestant country, were sensitive to accusations that they gave greater allegiance to a foreign pope than to American presidents. They reacted with a determination to be more patriotic than others. Catholics, for example, have provided a disproportionate number of top brass for the Pentagon. Now that they have come fully into the mainstream, this high degree of acceptance is threatened by the critical voices of their bishops who are speaking out on matters of peace and justice.

In many communities Roman Catholics and peace church members share counterculture bonds as they witness together for peace. They learn that the peace churches were born in civil disobedience. When Mennonites and Brethren baptized believers who had already been baptized as infants, they committed an illegal act punishable by death or exile. George Fox, an early Quaker leader, was in and out of jail many times. Refusing to swear oaths and kill Indians, these "peculiar people" constituted a small yet significant minority. These peace sects steadfastly insisted that a higher loyalty was due their Lord than any earthly power. This may well be one of their valuable ecumenical contributions. Finding a haven of religious freedom in William Penn's colony, they struggled to remain faithful to their calling while becoming respectable citizens in a democratic society. Often serving their neighbors and country so as to gain a high degree of respectability, today they are threatened when their own spiritual offspring challenge them to be faithful to their radical heritage.

Often a theology of the state has been derived from exegeting and reacting to interpretations of one text such as Romans

13. Pacifists have often teetered between Romans 13 and Revelations 13. The one chapter calls us to be subject to the powers. The other pessimistically names the empire as the beast. Duane Friesen, in an excellent brief study, demonstrates a wide variety of Mennonite responses to governments in the twentieth century.[1] He joins John Howard Yoder and other biblical scholars in proposing that a cluster of texts dealing with "powers and principalities" may provide a fuller and more adequate understanding of the state than any one text.[2]

> For we are not contending against flesh and blood, but against the principalities, against the powers, against the world rulers of this present darkness, against the spiritual hosts of wickedness in the heavenly places (Eph. 6:12).

The phrase, powers and principalities, appears several times in the Pauline and prison epistles. The current attraction to these texts may be partially the result of dashed hopes that a peaceful and more just society would come about through human progress in our century. There has been a growing awareness of the power of evil, the collective forces which transcend our own personal struggles and threaten the existence of civilization. Phrases like, "world rulers of the present darkness" and "spiritual hosts of wickedness in the heavenly places" seem to name a present reality.

Paul used the cosmological (angels and archangels), astrological and occultists language of his day. There is a growing consensus that this otherworldly language also related to institutions and ideologies of society. In the Pauline usage "powers and principalities" suggest invisible forces which break into our earthly existence. The world is thought of as being administered through angels. The state is only one of the earthly entities through which the powers manifest themselves. This biblical usage has parallels in the way we talk about "structures." There is the "power structure," "the structure of personality" or the "structure of a response." Structures which may be similar to those encompassed by these texts include religious, intellectual ('ologies and 'isms), moral (codes and customs) and political (courts, schools, race and nation) structures.

Powers Created As Good

He is the image of the invisible God, the first-born of all creation; for in him all things were created in heaven and on earth, visible and invisible, whether thrones or dominions or principalities and powers; all was created through him and for him. And he is before all things, and in him all things hold together (Col. 1:15-17).

Since so many of the texts refer to the powers in a negative way, it is good to begin with one which declares that they are a part of God's good creation. In Christ all the world powers hold together. Therefore we can positively affirm that structures in which humans relate to one another in orderly ways are good. Religious, intellectual, moral and social structures of some kind are a part of God's plan.

In talking with the Roman Catholics, I found myself confessing my patriotism in ways which surprised me. I have enjoyed the best America has to offer: a solid, pious middle class home, an excellent public school system, travel, camping, concerts, and the freedom of the broad plains. I grew up with a deep love for my country, I saluted the flag. I felt warm inside whenever Kate Smith sang "God Bless America." It was out of this background that I suffered a broken heart when my pacifist sensitivities helped me see that not all Americans lived this good life. Many blacks, other minority groups, and third world peoples were excluded.

From the doctrine of the creation of the powers, we learn basic biblical attitudes toward our government and society. We are to weep over the Jerusalems. We are to pray for the rulers. We are to honor the emperor. Reverence and worship, however, belong to God alone (1 Pet. 2:17). Some people beam in adoration when they are around those in high places. My temptation is the opposite. When I am around governors, senators or a president, I easily become self-righteous and look down my nose. But my faith calls me to relate to them as persons created in the image of God, as ones for whom Christ also died.

Some have the mistaken notion that it is unpatriotic to criticize the policies of one's nation. It is because we love our country, however, that we do not want it to go bankrupt or perish in a nuclear holocaust. If we love our children, we will not say yes to everything they do. We will be concerned when they are headed in the wrong direction. And so with our government. In a democracy which claims to covet the opinions of all the citizens, honest critical responses constitute the highest patriotism.

Theologians such as H. Richard Niebuhr have unfairly said that the peace churches are opposed to culture (Christ against culture). His analysis is based on the fact that conscientious objection to war conflicts with the highest values of the political community, namely, the virtue of dying in battle for one's country. This analysis overlooks the historic world-affirming nature of the peace church witness. The Mennonites from the beginning were concerned about refugees and about stewardship of the soil. Quakers tried to transform society in conformity to the Spirit of Christ. Living in the first nation to grant them religious liberty, the Dutch Mennonites were soon participating in the artistic, political, and educational life of Holland. Quakers led movements for prison reform and honesty in business dealings.

Some pacifists, carrying memories of persecution, did manifest separatist prejudices against other aspects of culture. Generally they were more reluctant to hold public offices, and when in office more reluctant to compromise their principles. Gradually, however, they permitted the holding of public office measured by criteria applied in the community of faith. This was the spirit of the answer given to a query brought to the Church of the Brethren Annual Conference in 1918:

> We recognize that, in a democracy, it is not wrong for Brethren to serve their communities and municipalities, to promote efficiency and honesty in social and civic life when the nonresistant principles and New Testament doctrines are not violated.[3]

Another basic guideline instructs members who hold public office to maintain close ties with the community of faith. Faithfulness to the church means openness to the counsel of brothers and sisters. Faithfulness to the gospel, while serving in the world, requires the support and prayers of the body.

Fall of the Powers

For I am sure that neither death, nor life, nor angels, nor principalities, nor things present, nor things to come, nor powers, nor height, nor depth, nor anything else in all creation, will be able to separate us from the love of God in Christ Jesus our Lord (Rom. 8:38).

And I saw a beast rising out of the sea . . . and to it the dragon gave his power and his throne and great authority. . . . Men worshiped the dragon for he had given his authority to the beast, and they worshiped the beast . . . (Rev. 13:1,2,4).

Though created by God to be good, human structures are fallen. The powers which were created to be agents of God's purposes in the world, now seek to separate us from the love of God. They have rebelled against their original role. Though we should be subject to those values and structures which are necessary to life and society, their absolute, idolatrous claims enslave us. The state becomes the beast when it demands for itself an allegiance which belongs to God alone. Though we cannot live without the powers, as Christians, we often have a difficult time living with them.

Both of my grandfathers were named Samuel, affectionately known as Uncle Sam, a familial greeting bestowed upon beloved elders in pioneer communities on the plains. My relationship with a third "Uncle Sam," has been marked by patriotic attraction and bitter disappointments. A most traumatic experience occurred during a session at the previously mentioned center for intercultural dialogue in Mexico. We listened to the story of a soldier who had escaped from El Salvador. He had been nonpolitical, not pleased with the violence of either the army or guerrillas. Then, he was drafted into the army. Informed that he would be fighting alien communists he found himself commanded to kill people just like his own family. When he had an opportunity, he escaped. The most horrid story he related was about a training session in torture. At a meeting in which a 13 year old girl was slowly tortured before their eyes, they were told not to let it bother them. For they were not killing a human being, but an animal, a communist. A sense of shame came over us when he identified the instructor as an officer in the U.S. army.

Though the young man's story seemed authentic, it could be false. I did not want to believe it. During the Democratic convention in 1968, I spent three days on the streets as an observer for the American Friends Service Committee. I was deeply shaken when I discovered that Brethren believed the official report of the city of Chicago about what had taken place more readily than mine. Why, I wondered, would Christians believe a mayor of a corrupt political machine over the report of a brother in Christ? I came to realize that Brethren, like a majority of Americans, did not want to believe the first reports of police brutality. They basically wanted to believe the best about their country and the worst about the demonstrators.

All peoples are tempted by collective self-righteousness. Individuals who do not feel their own worth identify with the righteousness and superiority of their nation. Collective self-righteousness assumes that the location of evil is somewhere else. The peace churches tell the world what my mother always told me: it takes two to fight. All of the sins do not lie on one side. The Bible calls us liars if we deny we have sin. We are guilty of blasphemy if we say our nation has no sin. We can join the popular preachers of our day in calling for repentance of individual sins. We dare not, however, join in their silence about the sins we commit together. The pervasive self-righteousness of our nation denies the biblical doctrine of justification by faith. Biblical realism forces me to listen to the account of the young soldier and to admit that such atrocities are indeed likely. We are not true parents or patriots if we overlook the worst actions of our own. True faith and hope do not come from looking the other way but from looking in the mirror and repenting of our sins.

Pacifists often react to the sins of their own countries by naively glorifying other nations. In some circles all the evil lies in Washington while the Soviets represent true righteousness. Our primary obligation is to repent of our own sins rather than thanking God we are not like other nations. We are to remove the beams from our own violent society before attempting to extract the specks from others. Nevertheless, biblical realism calls us to recognize the fallenness of all the powers.

And the same honest assessment should apply to each of us, even pacifists. Dale Aukerman offers a moving personal testimony:

> I acknowledge my own tendency to make of my No to war and my pacifism the key confirmation of my righteousness over against the unrighteousness of those who align themselves with or assent to the military. This tendency can disfigure me as it has often disfigured anti-war and peace movements. I need to be reminded again and again of the dark continuity between me and the men of the Pentagon, between me and the church people who bless the cursed weapons. . . There is no achieved righteousness of my own for countering that peril. There is only the One who, as in that Temple scene, interposes himself between me and the onslaught of doom and is leading me with others out of it.[4]

In spite of these necessary correctives, we are called to echo the prophetic ministry of our Lord: "Repent ye [of blasphemous and nationalistic self-righteousness], for the kingdom [of peace and righteousness] is at hand" (Matt. 3:2). Our preaching must flow from our deep love for our country and the world. Our judgment must reflect the judgment of God which falls upon the proclaimers as well as the fallen principalities. With Jonah we are called to preach repentance to the Ninevehs of our day because of God's great love and compassion for the world.

We may be called to say "No" to the principalities of death by saying "Yes" to life. Like Jesus in the temple, we may need to call a structure a den of thieves in order to say that it should be a house of prayer. There may be times when we must obey God rather than women or men. All of the peace churches have at some time in their history and teaching made a case for civil disobedience. Members are advised to keep the following in mind. Civil disobedience should only be undertaken after legal means to correct injustice have failed. Its spirit should be positive, not negative and militant. Loving dialogue with civil authorities should precede and continue during acts of disobedience. Christians should always adhere to nonviolence, avoiding harm and minimizing inconvenience to others. Christ's example shows us that we must be willing to pay the price of our witness.[5] It is possible to be subject to the powers without being obedient to them. Such was the case with draft resisters who submitted with respect and cooperation to the legal system, while at the same time refusing to obey laws requiring them to become a part of structures devoted to death and destruction.

God's Sovereignty Over the Powers

Let every soul be subject unto the higher powers. For there is no power but of God; the powers that be are ordained by God (Rom. 13:1, KJV).

For God sent the Son into the world not to condemn the world, but that the world might be saved through him (Jn. 3:17).

Ah. Assyria, the rod of my anger, the staff of my fury (Isa. 10:5).

Romans 13:1 is consistent with other texts in claiming that, in spite of their fallen condition, the powers are still under the providential rule of God. Though far from God-like in its behavior, the wicked empire could be named God's rod and staff. God was not gleefully punishing the children of Israel; they had brought the punishment upon themselves. But God was actualizing anger, for Assyria was allowed to wreak vengeance on God's people. In mysterious ways, God works for good through this human mess. In a biblical sense the wrath of God is an expression of God's love, the kind of patience and love which will allow us to go to hell if we are so determined.

Since we are created in the image of God, this means that God grants us freedom to relate or to rebel. The most basic meaning of the Greek word for power, *exousia*, is possibility of action. When God confers power to the Son, to the beast in Revelation, God grants freedom, the authority to act. Similarly we need a more correct understanding of the word *tetagmenai* (*tasso*) which in the King James text is translated "ordained." The root meaning of this word is "to put in order." The powers are not ordained by God in the sense that whatever they do is in accordance with the divine will. Rather God orders them, puts them in their place and lines them up according to divine purpose. In the Joseph story (Gen. 50:20) God did not ordain the brothers to do evil. Nevertheless, the story informs us that though the brothers did mean to do evil against Joseph, God used the situation for good. The fallen structures can serve the preserving patience of God as the arena for divine activity.

An examination of the key words does not support the prevalent misuse of Romans 13 in Protestantism. It has been a proof text for bestowing divine sanction on existing governments. Nations have been regarded as orders of creation which retain their divine status regardless of what they do. The meanings of the words "power" and "order" lend more support to Bonhoeffer's view, which emerged in his struggle with fascism. He wrote about orders of "preservation." God orders governments to preserve creation, to maintain order by supporting the good and opposing the evil. If in their fallenness, however, earthly powers destroy rather than preserve the possibilities of orderly existence, they truly become embodiments of spiritual hosts of wickedness in high places.

Consistent with this analysis is the interpretation many make of concluding verses of this passage (Rom. 13:7-8), which call us to pay respect where respect is due and give honor where honor is due. Then Paul adds that we owe no one anything, except to love one another. Here the apostle seems to suggest that Christians must discriminate. "Render to each his due" cannot be assumed to mean that we are to do whatever the government asks. It probably means that we should discern together what belongs to Caesar and what belongs to God. Since "nothing is due to anyone except love (verse 8)," the claims of Caesar are to be measured by whether they help us love our neighbors and allow us to fulfill the law of love. Romans 13:1-6 is placed between two love passages. Because Christians are told in 12:9 never to avenge themselves, there is no strong basis to interpret Romans 13 in a way which requires Christians to take up the sword.

It is time to place the interpretation of Romans 13 in the context of the doctrine of redemption. We have noted the biblical view that powers and principalities are created to be good. We can affirm those things that are good. But often the good is perverted and we behold the fallenness of the powers. In spite of the fall, God can still use them for good. But God desires their redemption. It is surprising how many people regard John 3:16 as the golden text of the Bible and ignore John 3:17. "God sent the son into the world, not to condemn the world, but that the world might be saved through him."

If we truly accept Jesus Christ as Saviour and Lord, we will know that personal commitment is part of his redeeming activity in the world. This brings us to ongoing issues in the Reformed-Anabaptist debate. Those who call for the strategy of the Reformed tradition believe Christians should participate aggressively in the structures of the world. They should be leaven transforming them according to God's will for justice and peace. Unashamedly we must enter politics, penetrating power structures. We must hold key offices and influence the decision-making process of leaders. Reformed activists criticize Anabaptists for refusing to get their hands dirty in order to make necessary compromises. Because of their church-world dualism, it is believed that Anabaptists shirk their responsibility of participating in God's redeeming activity in fallen structures.

In this debate Anabaptists answer first by noting the perils of the Reformed position. There are the dangers which come from compromise. Christians have often entered the political arena with high ideals of transforming society. In order to gain office, however, they compromise basic convictions for the sake of the future good which can be accomplished. Then they keep compromising in order to stay in office. Before long the visionary Christian is indistinguishable from other politicians. Even Quakers, it is argued, have not been all that different when they have occupied the highest office of the land.

Another peril is that of theocracy. When the church has controlled the power structures, it has been tempted to impose its beliefs and morality on all. Rather than trying to control the structures to make things come out right, Anabaptists have proposed the servant role—serving the powers and attempting to persuade the powers to conform more to the way of Christ.

The debate is helpful for all peacemakers. Is it too naive to hope that we could be half Reformed and half Anabaptist? In some ways, the Quakers already model this. The degree of the fallenness of the powers will vary. From time to time, however, those who participate in God's concern for the powers will be called to participate both inside and outside of the structures for the sake of redemption. Where we discern a kind of divine work within the structures, we can become a part of it while remaining firmly rooted and disciplined in the community of faith. On the other hand there are times when the powers are so incorrigible that we should refuse to collaborate in order to take sides with those who are oppressed. This refusal does not necessarily mean a retreat from society. Rather, it can be a major negative intervention within the process of social change.

The Work of Christ in Disarming the Powers

And you, who were dead in trespasses and the uncircumcision of your flesh, God made alive together with him, having forgiven us all our trespasses, having cancelled the bond which stood against us with its legal demands; this he set aside, nailing it to the cross. He disarmed the principalities and powers and made public example of them, triumphing over them in it [the cross] (Col. 2:13-15).

Since our lostness consists in our subjection to the rebellious powers of a fallen world, our salvation will mean freedom from and victory over the powers. The powers cannot simply be set aside or ignored. Rather their sovereignty must be broken. This early epistle tells us that this is what Jesus did on the cross. Here were the powers of religion and state crucifying Jesus, nailing him on a tree. And we are told that in this act Christ disarmed the powers.

How can that be? For Jesus was subject to the powers and submitted to their worst brutalities. Nevertheless he broke their rules by refusing to bow before their self-glorification. This is why they killed him. We have to do with One who is not the slave of any power, law or custom, community or institution, value or theory. Not even to save his own life would he become a slave to the powers. Christ disarmed the powers and principalities of their chief weapon, their ability to convince him that they were his primary security.

None of the rulers, either the Pharisees, Pilate or the scribes understood God's way. Because they crucified the true Lord, they are unmasked as false gods. They are made a public spectacle. Christ "has triumphed over them." This exposure of the powers by the scene on the cross was already their defeat. Yet this only comes visible as believers experience the resurrection. "The resurrection manifests what was already accomplished at the cross: that in Christ God has challenged the Powers, has penetrated into their territory, and has shown that He is stronger than they."[6]

Three ideas may be derived from the three phrases Paul used to describe what the death of Jesus did to the powers. He, *"made a public example of them."* I have thought about this when cartoonists sketch gross caricatures of our presidents or when we bad mouth our public leaders. It is certainly wrong to say degrading things about people whoever they are. In reality, however, public figures become corporate personalities. I have never known any of our presidents. I do not know whether I would like them, if I did. Could the text which says we do not struggle against flesh and blood mean that we do not oppose individual leaders, but the powers they embody and obey? We do not struggle against the Roosevelts, the Nixons, the Carters or the Reagans but against fallen angelic beings, the spiritual hosts of wickedness they obey, the collective fallen spirit of the people which says: "American first," "Whatever serves the selfish interests of America is good," "We are so right and they are so wrong that we are prepared to drop bombs on them." In reality it is not a president we oppose but the powers, the pervasive, fallen and collective spirits which enslave by motivating fears that foster hatred rather than love.

After stretching the first phrase to apply to political leaders, the second phrase applies to fears we have of our political enemies. We are told that *Christ triumphed over the powers* on the cross. If we really believe this, why do we need to be paranoid about Communism? I do not suggest that we should overlook the fallen nature of communist regimes. At one time the Soviets murdered 40,000 priests as a part of the attempt to destroy Christianity. Christians have faced brutal and subtle forms of persecution. They have had to deal with an abundance of anti-religious propaganda. Nevertheless, it has been impossible to stamp out Christianity. We need not imbibe the strong paranonia of multitudes of American Christians toward the Soviet Union. There, as well as here, the future belongs to Jesus Christ. The gospel has more power than marxist ideology, and the church will outlast the most zealous political movements. Dale Aukerman gives us pause when he proposes the real possibility that if churches are destroyed in the Soviet Union, it may well be by bombs made by Bible-believing Christians in America rather than by communists in the Soviet Union.

The punch line, Christ *disarmed the principalities and powers*, applies to our political situation. Jacques Ellul believes that people in modern states, including the United States, the Soviet Union, and his own native France live under a combination of three kinds of powers: administrative power, state power, and the power of the military-industrial complex. These powers which we created, now exist as real powers that control us more than we control them. In his book, *The Political Illusion*, Ellul maintains that it is an illusion to think that the political process or any politician can make a difference. As a sociologist, lawyer, former mayor and activist in the French resistance movement against the Nazis, he makes a persuasive case. When some people encounter his thesis and believe it, they become disillusioned. They feel immobilized. But they miss his basic point. A deeply committed Christian, this former marxist is simply proclaiming the gospel truth that we should place our ultimate faith in God rather than the political process. If our security is with God, then we will be freed to participate more effectively in the political process.

Christ disarmed the powers and principalities of their chief weapon which was and continues to be their ability to convince people that they are the divine regents of ultimate certainty, and that their bombs and armies provide our chief security. But if we recognize that our true security is in Christ and his way, the chief weapon has been taken from the powers. They have lost their grip. Wherever the cross is preached, the powers are disarmed. Those who have been reconciled through the cross are freed from the idolatry of the powers and are free to serve through the love that casts out fear.

The Work of the Church and the Powers

Of this gospel I was made a minister according to the gift of God's grace which was given me by the working of his power. To me, though I am the very least of all the saints, this grace was given, to preach to the Gentiles the unsearchable riches of Christ, and to make all men see what is the plan of the mystery hidden for ages in God who created all things; that through the church the manifold wisdom of God might now be made known to the principalities and powers in the heavenly places (Eph. 3:7-10).

After Christ, the church itself should be a sign and a token to the powers that their dominion has come to an end. Our resistance to the gods of this age will be fruitless unless we demonstrate in the community of faith how we can live freed from the powers. To reject nationalism, we must begin by recognizing that it was for all persons that Christ died on the cross. We can only resist social injustice if justice and mercy prevail in our common life. Only as the church is truly the church will it have much to say to the structures of the society.

A most significant text is often overlooked in discussions about the nature of the state. James and John were seeking special places next to Jesus in the coming kingdom. The other ten grew angry. In response Jesus contrasts the style of leadership of secular rulers with the servant role of his own disciples: "You know that those who are supposed to rule over the gentiles lord it over them, and their great men exercise authority over them. But it shall not be so among you: but whoever would be great among you must be your servant, and whoever would be first among you must be slave of all. For the Son of Man came not to be served but to serve, and to give his life as a ransom for many" (Mk. 10:42-45).

An effective social strategy is for the church to be a servant church. This view of the mission of the church has been named "candlelight ecclesiology." Simply by being the church, embodying concerns for peace and justice in its own life and ministries, it manifests the wisdom of God to the world. The church should be a countermovement or in Karl Barth's words, a provisional community, one which begins to manifest in its own life what God wants for the entire world. When structures of government fail to live up to their claims to serve people and, instead, demand that all be subservient to them, churches must generate structures which do serve.

Throughout history, expressions of "candlelight ecclesiology" have been one of the most successful ways of influencing the powers. In the Middle Ages monasteries took in boys and educated them because no one else was doing it. Church institutions and structures have started hospitals, orphanages, schools, homes for the elderly, universities, and many other charitable and humanitarian enterprises. Often, after the church demonstrates the need and value of such countercultural models, others see the light and found additional public institutions for the common good. The peace churches have known a more recent example. Their volunteer service programs were studied by the Kennedy administration as models for the Peace Corps and VISTA programs of the government. Some maintain that the church should be in the business of dreaming up alternative programs which might serve to reform or replace fallen structures and create new ones. Currently the Mennonites have been modeling a program that brings together victims and offenders for purposes of reconciliation and making things right. If it continues to be as effective as it appeared, similar programs may be adopted by the criminal justice system.

Old, tried and tested methods must not be neglected as strategies to make the manifold wisdom of God known to the powers and principalities. There is a need for biblical and prophetic preaching. The church through its rites and worship should publicly proclaim the good news of God's reconciling work on the cross so as to ordain us for ministries of reconciliation. The very existence of the church heralds the truth of its preaching. Christ is Lord over the powers from whose dominion the church has begun to be liberated. The preaching must deal with the fact that we remain pilgrims, exiles, and aliens in the world because of our allegiance to the coming kingdom. For this reason we need help in counting the cost of our nonconformity to the political faiths of our day. Above all the visions of the kingdom should be kept before us so we will participate in the signs and the first fruits of its coming. In an age of doomsday messages, the church must keep preaching the gospel of hope; a hope that does not turn away from the darkness but looks to the light shining in the darkness in expectation of surprising manifestations of peace and justice. Above all the church will keep alive the message that the source of our hope is God not the powers. If the church is to manifest the wisdom of God, it will not be through a Zealot-or a Herod-like stance. It will neither try to bring the powers to their knees nor collaborate with them to preserve the status quo.

In defining views toward culture, H. Richard Niebuhr proposed a typology which has become remarkably standard in ethical thought. He defined Christian movements as Christ of, above, against, and in paradoxical tension with/or transforming culture.[7] In his examples, he classified the peace church tradition as against culture. I have regarded this as unfair and would prefer a category he does not have at all; that is, Christ, the servant of culture. I believe this to be a more inclusive category, one which encompasses a variety of ways of witnessing that are consistent with the texts on powers and principalities. It is possible for the church to serve culture by:

—submitting to, honoring and praying for the powers;

—prophetically preaching the gospel of repentance to the structures;

—participating in the transformation of the structures;

—opposing structures where necessary;

—offering counterstructures where feasible;

—disarming the structures in preaching Christ crucified; and

—holding fast to the promises of God in spite of the powers.

I am indebted to John Howard Yoder's biblical studies on the powers. His own summary statement serves as a meaningful conclusion to the chapter.

The powers have been defeated not by some kind of cosmic hocus-pocus but by the concreteness of the cross; the impact of the cross upon them is not the working of magical words nor the fulfillment of a legal contract calling for the shedding of innocent blood, but the sovereign presence, within the structures of creaturely orderliness, of Jesus the kingly claimant and of the church who herself is a structure and a power in society. Thus the historicity of Jesus retains, in the working of the church as she encounters the other power and value structures of her history, the same kind of relevance that the man Jesus had for those whom he served until they killed him.[8]

8

Shalom Life Styles

On the evening of that day, the first day of the week, . . . Jesus came and stood among them and said to them, "Peace be with you." (Jn. 20:19)

He came and preached peace to you who were far off and peace to those who were near. (Eph. 2:17)

If possible, so far as it depends upon you, live peaceably with all. (Rom. 12:16).

Following the crucifixion the disciples stayed behind closed doors, discouraged, forlorn, and afraid of their enemies. Their resurrected Lord appeared. His first word to them in Aramaic or Hebrew was *shalom*. "Do not fear, all is well, everything is going to be all right." Here peace means well-being, salvation, and closeness in the new community. The author of the letter to the Ephesians named peace as the focus of the Lord's preaching, a message that broke down the dividing wall of hostility between those who were near and those who were far off, the Jews and the Gentiles. The various meanings of *shalom*—harmonious relationships, righteousness, justice, and peace—confirm that in the Judeo-Christian heritage there is no separation between personal and social ethics. As much as possible, live peaceably with all.

The Hebraic *shalom* places the accent on relational aspects of peace with God and one another. The Greek word, *eirene*, suggests harmony, coherence, and order. In Latin *pax* refers primarily to political peace between nations. Part of our confusion comes from having only one English word for all of these meanings. As peace studies programs emerge in academic circles, nearly every teacher argues that her or his course deals with peacemaking. Some advocate a more narrow definition of peace than others. They believe our times demand a special curriculum which focuses on issues of war and peace between nations. As the institution of slavery was eventually abolished, they reason, war as a method of settling disputes can and must be eliminated. This may or may not have much to do with how we raise our children or solve our problems in the church community.

The peace churches have related the peace witness to discipleship. *Shalom* is a way of life. In addition to saying no to war, *shalom* lifestyles apply the way of nonviolent love to everyday relationships. One of the students in the Doctor of Ministry program at our seminary, Greg Skiba, expressed it well in writing his vision of ministry:

> I envision my ministry as a life style wherein I come to grips increasingly with my own and other's participation in the sins and injustices we inflict on each other. When God's grace and forgiveness is experienced in this context, we are able to respond more gratefully with acts of compassion, justice and peacemaking. To truly live out of this experience and conviction would be, for me, just short of the kingdom.

The peace church heritage has taken shape in styles of spirituality, programs of mutual aid, workshops on family relationships, evangelistic strategies, studies in conflict resolution, resistance to violent structures, and numerous service ministries. Many members of the peace churches sing with gusto the popular song: "Let there be peace, and let it begin with me." In this chapter we look at areas in which *shalom* is found side-by-side with issues of war and peace.

Shalom Spirituality

I will never forget a night in the late sixties in Chicago with a group of draft resisters. Descending into a dingy basement, I encountered a motley assembly. They represented the counterculture, youth who were angry at society for attempting to force them to fight in an immoral jungle war halfway around the world. A surprise came at the end of the meeting. They joined hands. With tears streaming down some of their faces they sang: "Amazing grace, how sweet the sound, that saves a wretch like me!" I learned what some people may not realize even today. It was the draft resisters who kindled the popular revival of this old gospel song. In the thick of their fight against a sick society, they searched inwardly and discovered they were a part of the problem. In confession they sensed the amazing grace that forgives, accepts, and empowers.

Charles Finney was the chief catalyst for a revival movement that swept the American frontier in the decades immediately preceding the Civil War. Finney's "new measure" revivalism called for radical conversions and changed hearts. Moreover, it was expected that a personal acceptance of Christ as Saviour would immediately lead the converts to join some kind of reform society. There were abolitionist, temperance, and peace movements as well as societies to help prostitutes, preachers, or other victims of exploitation.

Whether it is radicalized resisters discovering a deeper faith or converted sinners joining social movements for reform, we discern the marriage of spirituality with social and political issues. Today, many of us are grateful that Roman Catholics are bringing their long tradition of spirituality to the peace movement. In this they serve the desire of many to root peacemaking in biblical faith, to conjoin meditation and action, to take both the inward and the outward journey.

From the beginning the Quakers did not make the separation that most Christians do between the spiritual and worldly. They were mystical and at the same time they were humanitarian. There were Quakers who had "great openings," moments of mystical insight that led to social action. Other Quakers, who never experienced such openings, nevertheless gained inner strength and conviction through their deep commitments to alleviate human suffering and eliminate wars.

A Quaker, Parker Palmer, has written unique observations about the inward and outward life in a Pendle Hill pamphlet entitled, *Escape and Engagement*. Using the analogy of a prisoner, he defines escape as freedom. In prayer we escape the rat race. Free from the shackles of conformity and security, we can envision life as it should be. Continuing to play with this analogy, Palmer reminds us that another word for "imprisonment" is "commitment." As we return to the world our commitment allows us to transcend the false gods of the social order—effectiveness, power, conformity—at the same time we serve the world. "So escape and engagement are complementary rhythms, not exclusive choices. They ebb and flow, wax and wane, each movement responding to the tuggings of the other."[1]

For Catholics and many others, Thomas Merton has embodied the Quaker emphasis of the inward and outward walk. One of the best known contemplatives in the twentieth century, this Trappist monk has probably been more responsible than any other American for the growing peace movement in Roman Catholicism. In his pilgrimage, his contemplative nature did not detach him from art, music, nature, sports, or the affairs of nations. For Merton, God was not that which is left when everything else is crossed off, but that which includes and embraces everything else.

The writings of Matthew Fox echo this.[2] He defines prayer as a radical response to life. "Radical" means to get to the roots, to take seriously that we are created in the image of God. Prayer is basically falling in love with life. Because prayer is a joyful response to the gift of life, we cannot help but be against all things that deny, destroy, and exploit life. In our affirmation of life, we affirm community formation and grow in our consciousness that community is worldwide.

Both Merton and Fox espouse a spirituality which, I think, is close to the experience of the Pietist forbears of the Brethren and of Martin Buber, the twentieth century popularizer of Hasidism (Jewish pietism). In spite of otherworldly motifs, they have a kind of devotion or mysticism that hallows all of life and creation.

Shalom Families

Though it might be possible to succeed in a worldwide movement against war without demonstrating exemplary life styles, the peace church tradition insists that our relationships in our families and communities should exemplify the peace we envision for the whole world. The peace witness should be conspicuous even in the way we treat our animals. Belief in the sacredness of life has led many pacifists to a more conservative stance on the issue of abortion. Pacifists who strive to love enemies and forgive seventy times seven should be more committed than others to work conscientiously to reconcile broken relationships in an era of quick-fix divorces.

Biblical teachings about peacemaking may be applied to the question of authority. Though the peace church tradition recognizes the necessity of order, structure, and authority, the heritage at its best is not compatible with some patriarchical and hierarchical views which are currently popular. In the New Testament, leadership abilities are named as gifts of Christ (Eph. 4:11). Leaders are called and given authority in order to promote the good of all. Jesus described authority patterns which were different from those of the Gentiles. Among them, rulers lord it over others and exercise great authority. With his disciples, he said, it is not to be that way. Rather, the greatest must be the servant of all (Mk. 10:35-45).

Is it possible to follow a way that is so radically different from common understandings in our world? Though New Testament scholars are not in agreement, some believe it is possible to reconcile this teaching with the household rules found in Ephesians 5:21-6:9. They sound hierarchical and perhaps reflect the culture of the time in instructing wives to be obedient to their husbands, children to obey their parents in everything, and slaves to be submissive to their masters in all respect. Some studies, however, demonstrate how different they are in comparison to popular Stoic teachings of the day.[3] The opening verse calls for mutual submission. "Be subject to one another out of reverence for Christ" (vs. 21). John Howard Yoder writes that such subordination is revolutionary because the dominant parties in the relationships are also required to be submissive, acting out of reverence for Christ. Husbands are admonished to love their wives as Christ sacrificed himself for the church. Fathers are advised not to provoke their children. And masters are commanded to treat their slaves fairly and justly.

Another way of speaking of this kind of submission is to stress that it is voluntary. My wife has at times reacted to what I have regarded as legitimate feminist emphasis on self-worth. For her, warnings not to live for and through one's husband and children have seemed to deny the basic Christian message that we are to live for others. I reply that service, if performed because it is expected or forced, is not what Jesus or Paul had in mind. Living for others becomes truly Christian when it is voluntary, arising out of the affirmation of one's freedom and personhood.

This accent on Christian freedom permeates the biblical message. In Christ, Christians of the first century no longer felt subordinate to any human power. Their experience of the new creation, the Christian community, led them to believe that their status had been changed. No longer were there Jew or Greek, slave or free, male or female, but oneness in Christ Jesus (Gal. 3:28). This call to mutual and voluntary subordination would not have been needed if authority had not been abused. This passage is consistent with the admonitions of Paul in his correspondence with the Corinthians. Concerning food offered to idols (1 Cor. 7), we are free as Christians to eat or not to eat. Yet, for the sake of the brother or sister, Paul calls for voluntary abstinence when lack of the same would offend.

Rigid structures that give unquestionable divine sanction to authority whether to a ruler or to a father threaten the gains made by the peace church tradition. Our fathers and mothers in the faith suffered torture, imprisonment, exile, and death because they would not compromise their obedience to Christ. The application of the higher allegiance principle even in family relationships is what Jesus clearly meant in saying that he came to bring a sword instead of peace:

> For I have come to set a man against his father, and a daughter against her mother, and a daughter-in-law against her mother-in-law; and a man's foes will be of his own household. He who loves father or mother more than me is not worthy of me; and he who loves son or daughter more than me is not worthy

of me, and he who does not take up his cross and follow me is
not worthy of me (Matt. 10:35-38).

This is certainly not a statement against striving for *shalom* type
relationships in the family circle. It is a strong affirmation, however, that our loyalty to Jesus Christ takes precedence over all
other relationships. Though we are not promised that in placing
Jesus first, all will be well, we are promised that in all of life and
particularly in families losing our lives for the sake of Jesus will
mean that we ultimately find them.

Shalom Evangelism

Evangel, gospel, good news all mean the same thing. Evangelism refers to both the nature and proclamation of the gospel.
The New Testament expresses in a variety of ways the scope of
the good news. The writers speak of the gospel of the kingdom,
the gospel of God, the gospel of Jesus Christ, the gospel of the
glory of Christ, the gospel of salvation and the gospel of peace.
In Acts 10:36 Peter spoke of God preaching the word to Israel,
namely, "the good news of peace through Jesus Christ (he is
Lord of all)." Paul encouraged the Ephesians to shoe their feet
with the equipment of the gospel of peace (6:15). The gospel of
Jesus Christ, of salvation, is the same as the gospel of peace.

We take away from the glory of the good news if we attempt
to reduce the meaning to one facet of the biblical message. It
would be wrong for pacifists to reduce the content of the good
news to the gospel of peace. But too often the good news of
peace has been omitted from proclamations of the gospel or
reduced to an inner calm of good conscience. In many circles
peace has been completely separated from the gospel. The good
news is forgiveness of sins, the joy of being accepted as children
of God and the promise of eternal life. These are all basic to the
gospel. However, the good news of peace has often been second-
ary, a fruit of the gospel instead of an integral part of the gospel.
The danger of this kind of separation is that the good news is
often presented as salvation from the world instead of for the
world. It can easily lead to a preoccupation with saving one's

own soul and overlooking the call to participate in God's reconciling activity in the world.

Peace with God and peace with others cannot be separated. Both make up the content of the good news. Both need to be proclaimed in the ministry of evangelism. It is good news that God has made peace with us through the cross, but it is also good news that Christ has broken down the dividing walls of hostility between peoples. The King James translation of 2 Corinthians 5:17, "if any man be in Christ, he is a new creature," is a good rendition if we add the more accurate translation of the New Jerusalem Bible: "And for anyone who is in Christ, there is a new creation." It is good news that reconciliation with Christ brings both a new person and a new community into being. Our contemporaries continue to long for personal acceptance. But those who suffer from paranoid fears of the Russians and idolatrous trust in military might also need the good news that Christ is our strength and refuge. His love casts out all fear.

Raymond Fung, evangelism director of the World Council of Churches, has called attention to the forgotten side of evangelism. We are well aware that evangelism is the preaching of good news to sinners, but he says we have neglected the fact that the gospel is also good news to those who have been sinned against. He tells about taking a textile worker to church with him in Hong Kong. After the service they went out for lunch. The feedback was this: "Well, the sermon hit me. And you know, what the preacher said is true. I am lazy, I have a violent temper, and I am addicted to cheap entertainment. I guess he was talking about me." Fung reported his excitement. The worker continued: "But nothing was said about my boss. Nothing about how he employs child laborers, how he doesn't give us legally required holidays, how he puts on false labels, how he forces us to do overtime." Fung observes that the sermon spoke well to this man's sins but not to his sinned-againstness. All of which is to say that both the call to personal repentance and to justice is a part of the good news of inviting people to accept Christ as Saviour and Lord.

Since both personal and social peace are integral to the gospel, it is difficult to find biblical support for many of our neat schemes. They are often good and helpful but seldom do justice to the fulness of the biblical message. A common scheme calls us to accept Jesus Christ as personal Savior first, then peace-making will follow as a fruit of our conversion. If we change the hearts of individuals, it is claimed, the world will automatically be transformed. However, if peace is not regarded as a part of the gospel, it is easy for so-called born-again Christians to be ready to launch missiles of mass destruction if so commanded, without any thought that this might be contrary to the gospel. This separation of personal from social salvation made it possible for Bible-believing slave traders to conduct daily devotions on ships carrying human cargo like cattle.

Christian experience belies neat schemes for coming to Christ. Some make a deep personal commitment before understanding fully the gospel of peace. Others are moved by the spirit of compassion of our Lord and thereby are led to personal affirmations of faith. Some cry "Lord! Lord!" and then do the will of God. Others do the will of God and then come to acknowledge Christ as lord over all of life. Henry Cadbury, Quaker professor at Haverford College, was suspended for writing a letter to a newspaper decrying the vengeful spirit and the punitive proposals of the American peace plans for Germany following World War I. His letter brought the college under fire, and the board met and suspended him. Not one member of the board spoke on his behalf. After this trial by fire, Henry Cadbury told a friend that he had not known how deeply he felt until he acted. Thereafter, he often shared from his own experience that action might lead to deeper faith just as often and as easily as belief leads to action. This may be very similar to the biblical truth which Bonhoeffer captured in his much-quoted statement from *The Cost of Discipleship*: "only he who believes is obedient, and only he who is obedient believes."[4]

Shalom Conflict

It may seem a bit ridiculous to talk about peaceable conflict. The apostle Paul, however, suggests this. In advising the Ephesians to speak the truth with their neighbors, he admonishes them that even when angry, they are not to sin; for the sun should not go down on their anger (4:25-27). Similarly, the peace church tradition has lived by the assumption that it is not the most horrible thing to have conflicts; sooner or later they are bound to happen. The important thing is how we deal with them. Matthew 18:15-20 very early became basic to the peace groups; for the text offers a practical yet profound methodology for settling disputes. If your brother or sister sins against you, go to him or her. If this does not work, draw two or three others into the conversation. And if he or she still refuses to listen, go and tell it to the church. For generations the Brethren regularly read this passage at the time of baptism. As these admonitions became deeply imbedded in their consciousness, it was natural that biblically informed and common sense versions of conflict resolution became a part of Brethren teaching and life.

It follows that the peace churches have nurtured social scientists who have become leaders in the growing fields of mediation, communication, and resolution of conflicts. A Brethren, Ron Arnett, has creatively integrated his own speciality in communications with insights from philosophy, psychology, sociology and with wisdom from veteran pacifists. His timely and unique book is entitled: *Dwell in Peace: Applying Nonviolence to Everyday Relationships*.[5] Such integration of the peace heritage with contemporary insights is producing specialists with the competency to deal with eruptions in congregational life.

Mennonites have helped to give birth to VORP (Victims and Offenders Reconciliation Program). Several successful efforts have brought victims of crimes face to face with offenders, as in the following typical scenario. A burglar attempts to explain his or her behavior to a person who in turn tells how it feels to find one's house in complete disarray. In cooperation with the legal system, the offender agrees to make things right by mowing the victim's lawn for several months. In the process they meet often enough to learn to know each other and in some cases establish helpful friendships.

Conflict resolution literature frequently features principles in harmony with the spirit of Matthew 18. First, it is necessary to confront the person who offended or sinned. In our life together we often deal with conflict by adopting a permissive attitude: "Let everybody believe or do his or her own thing." Such an expression of individualism not only reveals a lack of vision for the church and society, but it also can be a sign of indifference. We may not care enough to confront.

Another common approach to conflict has been to pretend we do not have it. Many congregations repress their differences for the sake of unity and add even more pressure to the boiling pot. The steam then escapes in unexpected places. Eventually the lid blows off. Other congregations do not "have problems" because strong authority figures speak the last word. We have seen, however, how such leadership can violate people as well as biblical views of authority.

In our attempts to confront honestly, we need to examine both our motives and our goals. Sometimes we are determined to defend our reputation or the purity of the church. Some seek out offenders in order to preserve community standards or demonstrate the seriousness of sin. Some may be motivated by a desire to punish or avenge. The Bible, however, suggests we should have in mind the good of the person being confronted. Our mission is to forgive, and the reason to forgive a sister or a brother is that God has forgiven us.

The reconciliation passage in Matthew 18 is preceded by the teaching of Jesus that it is not the will of God that one weak member should perish. It is followed by Peter's inquiry as to how many times we are to forgive. The answer is shocking and offensive: "I do not say to you seven times, but seventy times seven" (V.22). The chapter ends with a parable of forgiveness and a severe warning to those of us who do not forgive our brothers and sisters from the heart (V.35). Even the command to treat another person as a Gentile or a tax collector when that person refuses to listen to the church must be carried out in the spirit of our Lord. For Jesus ate with tax collectors and was known to be their friend.

These principles point to the value of the second step in dealing with conflicts in Matthew 18. We do need other witnesses to check our motivations as well as to facilitate the process of reconciliation. This should not, however, keep us from taking the first step. Positively, some of my warmest relationships have been with people who confronted me or with whom I was honest in a Matthew 18 type of encounter. Negatively, I sometimes find myself avoiding Matthew 18 because of the great amount of time that may be involved. Nevertheless, in personal relationships it has been demonstrated that there is no easy reconciliation apart from some kind of judgment and the agony of suffering love.

This truth is also applicable in the social realm. We often think it would be nice if blacks and whites would simply start loving one another and know a painless integration. We want to bypass the occasions in which blacks honestly tell us that our idea of integration, their becoming like us, violates who they are. We need to hear some of the ways they do not want to be like us. They need to share the pride they have in their own history. We need to hear them assert that they want more control over the institutions which shape their lives. Only then can we gather around the tables as equals.

Most Americans believe that confrontive actions increase rather than decrease hatred and division. This was the charge against Martin Luther King when he marched through the Chicago neighborhoods. Critics of King maintained that he was creating more prejudice and backlash by arousing the anger of whites. He did not agree. He maintained that the marches flushed out the prejudices which were already there. King believed the racism that northerners always attributed to southerners and not to themselves needed to come to the surface. Only then could the prejudices be acknowledged, confessed, and dealt with as an essential step on the way to reconciliation.

Tax Resistance
A Case Study in Shalom Life Styles

The question of tax resistance is a current controversial issue where our ability to be honest and loving will be tested. It may be a passing fad, one that will quickly date this book. I am following an opposite hunch, however. It may be a debate that will be with us for some time. Historically, the peace churches have disagreed on this issue from the beginning. I write, desiring to be as fair as possible, at the same time confessing my bias as a tax resister. My purpose in discussing this issue is not to make a logical proof case for or against tax resistance. Rather, it is to point to a unity behind the differences. In the pacifist tradition when we are at our best, both sides argue from *shalom*-like assumptions.

Many pay war taxes without thinking because they have to. We may pay some taxes because we want to. But what about war taxes? Those persons I know best, who make the case for paying all taxes, do so out of a desire to apply the gospel of peace in their everyday lives. They believe they have the Bible on their side. There are several texts that explicitly imply such approval. Paul advised Christians at Rome to pay taxes to an empire that spent large amounts of money for military purposes. Moreover, paying taxes is consistent with the nonresistant life style that Jesus taught. If a government official, soldier or otherwise, forces you to go one mile to carry mail or equipment, do not resist. Instead, willingly go the extra mile. Why create problems with the state over money that it is going to get anyway, sometimes with additional penalties and interest? Although one's life belongs to God, it is permissible to give back to Caesar what Caesar created and what bears his image.

These persons accurately observe that some tax resisters violate the nonresistance stance, acting out of anger rather than love. In a movement for world peace, it is wrong to foster a warlike spirit. There are more constructive ways to witness to one's faith than to attempt to change the system through manipulative tactics. They often see tax resisters as self-righteously condemning the violence of the state while manifesting a violent spirit toward the state.

Not all, but some, who make this case stress that the state operates outside the perfection of Christ. Therefore, the sword has been approved by God for the state but not for the Christian. But it is permissible for Christians to pay taxes in cooperating with the divine mandate to have an orderly society in which the wicked are punished and the innocent protected.

Tax resisters are at one with other pacifists in believing that Christian participation in war is contrary to the will of God. For them, however, the same reasons which lead to refusing to give our bodies for war lead to withholding money from taxes for genocidal weapons. They take the stewardship teachings seriously that they learned in Sunday school. Money represents the fruit of our labors, our very lives, and should be dedicated to God. Consequently, they feel deep pain in realizing that members of peace churches give many times the amount given for all charitable and church programs to pay for the military portion of the federal budget.

Often feeling immobilized in the face of the gross misuse of the resources God has given us, tax resisters believe a good place to begin is with ourselves. Though far from a perfect witness without temptations, resistance to taxes is one way of strongly expressing concerns about the immorality of our national priorities. It is a concrete public witness to our affirmation of life and to Christ's love for the world which he came to redeem. Instead of placing the burden of our peace witness on eighteen-year-old youth responding to the draft, tax resistance provides an opportunity for those who are older to count the cost of nonconformity in risking penalties of the law.

Moreover, tax resisters do not believe the texts command the payment of all taxes. Jesus did not respond to the question of whether we should pay taxes with a simple yes. Following his statement about paying taxes in Romans 13, Paul may have introduced the principle of discrimination when he counseled the Romans to "pay taxes to whom taxes are due." There may be occasions when taxes are not due to Caesar. Tax resisters further derive such a possibility from Paul's final summary statement: "you owe no one anything, except to love one another." This love we also owe to the IRS. I can testify to many good relationships and conversations with Internal Revenue Service people, so much so that I often become defensive for them when I hear disrespectful remarks.

People on each side of the debate become distressed at the seeming self-righteousness of the other side. Tax resisters often judge others to be less faithful to the gospel of peacemaking. Advocates of the payment of all taxes rankle resisters by saying they are unbiblical and inconsistent. Though often disturbing, the debate has the possibility of contributing to our understanding of how and what it means to be faithful to Jesus Christ in an apocalyptic age.

Shalom Mythology

I do not use myth in the sense of something which is not true. Rather, myth is a story or a perspective which is held to be true even though the truth may not be absolutely verifiable. Such is the case with my personal story and the stories I was taught as a youth. I was nurtured in a subculture where people believed we should and could live by the Sermon on the Mount. The Pauline motto was engraved on a plaque on my bedroom wall: "Love never fails." Mother believed that. She frequently informed me that it takes two to make a fight. In church school we were told that the way to destroy an enemy was to make him your friend. My grandfather operated a little grocery store in Kansas in a pioneer setting where bandits were often a law unto themselves. He told me how they encircled his house on their horses, fired shots in his direction, and tried to frighten him into handing over the daily purse. For my Dunker grandfather, the moral of the story was that unarmed merchants survived with more money and lived longer than those who flashed their pistols in efforts to defend themselves.

It was natural that I became a political pacifist. The first sermon I preached was entitled: "Christianity Works," and was full of stories of how soft words had turned away the wrath of angry folk who had been violated by something I said or the way I drove. Like many others in my generation, I soon experienced a period of disillusionment with my neat mythology of love. I worked in an inner city settlement house in Chicago and learned that love does not always work. The bully might take the apple or baseball bat and throw it back in one's face. I sensed what I later learned from Kierkegaard. Love does not always elicit a response of love. Genuine love often evokes hatred. We hate a loving person because he or she often shows us who we really are. Society has consistently nailed to the cross those who live too far above the commonly accepted standards as well as those who live too far below them. I encountered Reinhold Niebuhr who maintained that those entrenched in power will seldom relinquish their privileged positions because of our smiles, loving approaches, or passionate sermons. Something more might be needed.

I came to a juncture. I could choose to follow my pacifist heroes, such as Ernest Lefever, out of the pacifist camp. They repudiated pacifism for the same reasons they had defended it, namely, from pragmatic political considerations. Or I could adopt what for me was a newly discovered Anabaptist position, one that emphasizes that pacifism is still the way for those who would be Christians even if this way leads to a cross. For a time I chose the second position which allowed me to espouse the pacifist witness as a personal life style while maintaining real doubts whether the Jesus way could be applied to political issues. It was helpful for me to discover that the motto on my bedroom wall should more accurately be translated, "love never ends." This allowed me to modify my stance, realizing that though love may temporarily fail, the nonviolent cross is the way that will ultimately triumph. For it is God's way. Unfortunately or fortunately, I have never been able to recover the neat pacifist package of my youth. My position is not neat. In spite of all I have written, I still struggle with hard and valid questions posed to pacifists.

As Americans we are very much aware of other stories in the history of our nation, mythologies that say we achieved independence by violent revolution, won the west through many shoot-outs with the Indians, and have been more secure when we have had guns in our holsters and bureau drawers. The mythology of violence is deeply ingrained in the American psyche. In the oft-quoted words of Rap Brown, "Violence is as American as apple pie." Nancy Reagan told a reporter how she always felt much better when she had a revolver at her bedside when her husband was away.

Through the thousands of violent deaths that our children view on television, they might easily believe that violence is effective. The good guys who shoot it out with the bad guys nearly always survive to come back and do the same thing next week. If the right people have the skill and weapons to kill, it is all right. This view is carried over into the arena of foreign relations. If we flex our muscles and make our battleships and might visible, we will gain the respect of the world. Guns and more armaments are the answer to the problems of the world whether in Central America, the Far East or the Middle East.

When sharing these two mythologies on college campuses, it has been helpful to point first to the pitfalls of my story. Then I follow by suggesting that the popular mythology also has problems. It may both soothe my soul and promote dialogue to examine questions relating to both mythologies. As it is important for peace people to become aware of the naivete and shallow assumptions behind certain brands of pacifism, so it is important to point out that our culture's infatuation with violence is based on faith that violence works with more effectiveness than the evidence supports. Quaker Gene Sharp has done extensive work examining nonviolent activity. In his detailed studies of the American revolutionary war, he documents the thesis that in events like the Boston Tea Party the nonviolent revolution was well underway. The colonists could have secured their freedom without firing a shot. He presents a persuasive case that the violent fighting actually prolonged the revolution. When examining something that might have happened but did not, historians, like all of us, are influenced by their faith perspectives. During the hostage crisis with Iran the United States attempted a rescue mission which failed miserably. Eight Americans were killed. The next morning a poll was taken. Americans not only approved the action but wanted their government to try the same thing again.

These stories illustrate that in basic perspectives we live by faith rather than by sight. As we learn from history, our faith determines where we look. One mythology looks to the rise of Hitler and reasons that had we been armed to the teeth, Hitler would not have dared to attack other nations. The other faith looks to the peace settlements of World War I and believes that if there had been stronger pacifist influence, statesmen would have avoided the unjust peace treaty that created the conditions which brought Hitler to power. Because our world is so complicated and interrelated, it is very difficult to calculate the consequences of our actions. We truly do walk by faith more than sight.

Of the two mythologies which do we choose? Neither one neatly answers the ambiguities, the complicated issues of our existence. By faith the peace church tradition believes one to be more consistent with the Jesus story and the practice of the early Christians. The popular myth is based on the will to power; the other is based on a will to serve. The one places trust in God. The other is seduced by a faith in power which may enfeeble, for in voting for huge armaments to scare the Russians, the nation becomes weaker and less secure. The other witnesses to the power of God made perfect through weakness (2 Cor. 12:9). It knows that when the Holy Spirit comes, there is power. The mythology of might is based on the fear of communism, the Russians. Faith in the nonviolent cross is based on the belief that perfect love casts out fear? (1 Jn. 4:18). Faith in violence conforms to the wisdom of our age. Faith in the way of suffering love confirms that God's foolishness is wiser and God's weakness is stronger than men and women. The one faith looks to the strong, the brilliant, the wealthy to make us secure. The other faith believes that the lowly, the poor, the meek will inherit the earth. The one mythology manifests the love of power. The other mythology believes in the power of love.

Epilogue

What If? Questions Asked of Pacifists

Pacifists have rightly been accused of oversimplifying issues. However, there is a feeling in peace circles that neither side possesses a monopoly on oversimplification. Nonpacifists ask: "What would happen if someone attacked your grandmother?" It is assumed that normal people would protect their grandmother. If the pacifist, then, can be forced to say that he or she is a normal, red-blooded American, the assumption is that the case for pacifism comes tumbling down.[1]

The questions and problems regarding pacifism are more involved than the usual superficial interrogation indicates. Folk musician Joan Baez makes this point beautifully in an excerpt from her autobiography. A participant in numerous protest, civil rights, and peace movements, she has remained a pacifist. Persons who have encountered the typical barrage of questions from draft board members, judges, Sunday school class members, bull session participants, and others will appreciate her satirical treatment, titled, "What Would You Do If?"

"OK, you're a pacifist. What would you do if someone were, say, attacking your grandmother?

"Attacking my poor old grandmother?"

"Yeah. You're in a room with your grandmother, and there's this guy about to attack her and you're standing there. What would you do?"

"I'd yell, 'Three cheers for Grandma!' and leave the room."

"No, seriously. Say he had a gun and he was about to shoot her. Would you shoot him first?"

"Do I have a gun?"

"Yes."

"No. I'm a pacifist, I don't have a gun."

"Well, say you do."

"All right. Am I a good shot?"

"Yes."

"I'd shoot the gun out of his hand."

"No, then you're not a good shot."

"I'd be afraid to shoot. Might kill Grandma."

"Come on. OK, Look. We'll take another example. Say you're driving a truck. You're on a narrow road with a sheer cliff on your side. There's a little girl standing in the middle of this road. You're going too fast to stop. What would you do?"

"I don't know. What would you do?"

"I'm asking you. You're the pacifist."

"Yes, I know. All right, am I in control of the truck?"

"Yes."

"How about if I honk my horn so she can get out of the way?"

"She's too young to walk. And the horn doesn't work."

"I swerve around to the left of her, since she's not going anywhere."

"No, there's been a landslide."

"Oh. Well, then. I would try to drive the truck over the cliff and save the little girl."

Silence.

"Well, say there's someone else in the truck with you. Then what?"

"What's my decision have to do with my being a pacifist?"

"There's two of you in the truck and only one little girl."

"Someone once said, 'If you have a choice between a real evil and a hypothetical evil, always take the hypothetical one.' "

"Huh?"

"I said why are you so anxious to kill off all the pacifists?"

"I'm not. I just want to know what you'd do if—"

"If I was with a friend in a truck driving very fast on a one-lane road approaching a dangerous impasse where a ten-month-old girl is sitting in the middle of the road with a landslide on one side of her and a sheer drop-off on the other."

"That's right."

"I would probably slam on the brakes, thus sending my friend through the front windshield, skid into the landslide, run over the little girl, sail off the cliff and plunge to my own death. No doubt Grandma's house would be at the bottom of the ravine and the truck would crash through her roof and blow up in her living room where she was finally being attacked for the first, and last, time."[2]

Hypothetical Situations

In this parody Joan Baez points to some fundamental assumptions. One is that no one knows exactly what he or she will do in moments of crisis. Such experiences often bring out the worst. Crisis situations also may bring out the noblest and best Christian response. Joan is also making the point that hypothetical questions deserve hypothetical answers, for hypothetical questions are set up in such a way as to manipulate the outcome. In the above case the hypothetical situation made it impossible for the pacifist to avoid killing one or more persons. Hypothetical alternatives are needed to demonstrate that the game can work both ways.

For example, you arrive suddenly on a terrible scene. A group of children are playing. A man is pointing a gun in their direction. If you shoot him, you will save the children. If you fail, you may be responsible for their death. You shoot. The man is dead. As long as it is hypothetical, however, why not add a bit more? There was a ferocious bear coming up the hill which the man could see and you could not. He was actually going to shoot the bear in order to save the children. Since your shot killed him, however, the bear mauled several children to their death. Tragically you only had one shot.

What If We Would All Disarm?

Though it might be fun to continue this kind of gamesmanship, it might be helpful to consider more seriously some of the other hypothetical questions posed to pacifists. This one is common: "What would happen if everyone laid down all arms?" One's first response is to exclaim, "Wonderful! This means that at last there would be peace in the world." It is protested that the question has been phrased wrongly. "What if all Americans became pacifists? Would not the Russians, Chinese, or others walk in and take us over?" From my personal acquaintance with Americans, it is very difficult to imagine all Americans ever becoming pacifists, but I have to treat the question as if such were possible.

It might be that the example of the most powerful nation in the world practicing the way of suffering love would have such an impact that the conquering armies could not be disciplined sufficiently to do their job, and world opinion would be aroused to stop the action. Or it might result in the most massive slaughter, martyrdom, and noblest witness to Christianity this world has ever seen. Or again it might mean Americans for the first time would have to live under the type of dictatorship which their money has helped to keep in power in Spain, South Vietnam, Philippines, Guatemala, and many other places in the world.

Frankly, I do not know what would happen if all of America became Christlike and took up the cross of suffering love. But I do know that the feelings of the questioner and the pacifist are based upon two entirely different assumptions. The questioner usually looks at the possibility of every American following in the steps of Jesus as the greatest tragedy possible. I think it would be wonderful. I cannot begin to predict what might take place. But I would like to see it happen.

What If Hitler?

What about Hitler? With the genocide of 6,000,000 Jews and the ruthless imposition of his dictatorship on many other countries, how could one fail to resist this type of evil? Such questions cannot be answered flippantly. We do not have here hypothetical case: Hitler actually existed, and we know about the horrors of the period. The question is most selective, however, in that it isolates one situation in history in order to make a case. A pacifist may be tempted to counter with a different case likewise anchored in history. For example, if America had been pacifist and had kept out of World War I, the world might never have known the unjust peace treaty and severe reparations which helped to create the conditions for Hitler to come to power. Another bit of speculation will indicate the way to plead a position by the type of "if" question selected. If America had not entered World War II, Germany and Russia might have destroyed each other to the extent that communism would have been crushed and Germany so weakened as to ease her stranglehold on Europe.

The question about Hitler may also presuppose too easily that the war brought about good results. The war made it possible for the Soviet Union to dominate Eastern Europe. After the war more peoples of the world came to live under totalitarianism than before. Many have observed that the losers, Germany and Japan, who were not allowed to spend their money on armaments, have consequently become better off economically than the winners. From my perspective this is not so bad. But it is bad that Hitler, though likely committing suicide, succeeded in forcing the losers to adopt some of his ways. The allies, who deplored the atrocities of the German Fuhrer, were responsible for the horrible firebombing of Dresden and the barbaric deed of dropping atomic bombs on Hiroshima and Nagasaki. And many feel that the erosion of sensitivity and scruples which became necessary to defeat totalitarian Germany, Italy, and Japan made it possible for a freedom-loving humanitarian democracy like the United States to drop napalm on children, defoliate thousands of acres of forests, and stage the worst bombing raids in history on the defenseless peoples of Laos, Cambodia, and Vietnam.

Such reasoning, however, begs the original question. Most

pacifists would advocate a loving resistance to Hitler, noble examples of which were in evidence in the underground movements of conquered Scandinavian countries. One dare not assume that such nonviolent resistance would have reduced the tyranny or even the suffering of the period. A Christian pacifist cannot promise that the way of the cross will be effective in any given situation. She or he cannot assume that the pacifist way will be widely accepted. There does remain the faith that the way of the cross is the right response and that, if it is tried, God may use it for the best of all. There is an attitude of patience involved here. One lives in the faith that evil regimes do have within themselves the seeds of their own destruction. There is evidence, for example, of several plots to overthrow Hitler's tyranny by his own officials. But one cannot depend on such political analyses. For we can never know the answer to the "what if" questions of the past or the future. We can trust in his way in hope that this is *the* way.

The same problem is raised today in a new form by persons who advocate violent revolution for dispossessed people under repressive regimes. It is argued that violent revolution is less violent than the present injustices. Institutionalized violence to persons can be more vicious than overt physical violence. For the former is perpetuated by the power structure in the form of psychological slavery, high infant mortality rates, poor medical care, ghetto-type living, and low life expectancy. Some say that China, which suffered through a ruthless violent revolution, is better off than India, where basic revolutionary changes have not come about and where widespread poverty, lack of land reform, and institutionalized violence are found. Such arguments by revolutionaries today are difficult to answer. The pacifist, however, lives in the faith that, in the long run, just means are more likely to gain just ends.

There is no pat way to deal with the hypothetical or the real questions asked of pacifists. It is obvious that some of the answers as well as the questions posed in this chapter have been contrived and superficial. We need a sense of humor. Sensitive to the total lives of our adversaries and open to new insights we may gain, we need to learn how to share in love what truth we may have. But witness we must—be it a silent presence or a prophecy of woe.

After pointing to the pitfalls of the hypothetical game, let me now yield to the temptation. "What if, one would come and choose as disciples among others, a few freedom fighters, a militant racist, and an official of the Internal Revenue Service? What if he would teach them that the way to overcome evil is with good? What if this same one would say he was going to set at liberty those who are oppressed? What if this preacher would return home and advocate in the home church that all farm land and property should be divided anew? What if this person would go into the churches of the land and turn over the offering plates which are filled with the profits from the military-industrial complex. What if?"

Nonviolent Action

Quaker Gene Sharp has done extensive research into the history and practice of nonviolent action. He claims that our society overlooks the failures of violent actions and glamorizes the successes of war and violence. Hypothetical questions are designed to point to the folly of nonviolent responses while we overlook numerous historical successes of nonviolence. His research documents many such successes such as the protest of teachers in Norway to Nazi rule and the demonstrations of spouses of Jews which gained release for their husbands. I have thought about his views with reference to Dietrich Bonhoeffer's participation in one of the conspiracy plots against Hitler. Numerous theologians have cited Bonhoeffer as one of the best examples to justify violent resistance. Yet this plot and others failed. As a result some 5,000 more persons died who might have lived. What if, I have conjectured, pacifists would cite such a failure to illustrate the validity of the nonviolent way? Four months after American hostages were placed in captivity at the Embassy in Iran (November 1979), our government attempted a rescue operation which was a miserable failure. Technical equipment failed. Six Americans were killed. Immediately, polls revealed that Americans, for the most part, not only favored what was called a "mission," but thought such an attempt should be tried again. If a dramatic nonviolent effort had failed, would it have been followed by pleas to try it again or would it have been publicized as a proof that we now need "to get tough"? The conclusion I derive from this is that we are not guided as much by evidence as by faith. Americans and others have more faith in violence than nonviolence. This faith is cultivated by a mythology that wars have preserved and defended freedom and by a steady television diet in which violent actions make things come out right. The "good guys and gals" keep living so as to return for next week's escapades even though they are slugged, shot at, and in mortal danger again and again. Gene Sharp calls us to make much greater efforts to tell stories and examine situations, hypothetical and otherwise, which point to the power of nonviolence.

Concluding Observations

In raising hypothetical questions, many persons make a direct application from one's personal action to one's stance on the question of war. If one believes in defending his wife, it is assumed that he should believe in a defensive war. Even if a pacifist would defend her husband, this does not mean that she would immediately move to bomb the attacker's spouse and relatives. More important is the point that such reasoning overlooks the fact that some pacifists advocate police action for the state but still oppose all wars. They make a distinction between coercive action against the guilty individual from whom society needs to be protected and the wholesale killing of the innocent with the guilty in modern warfare.

Pacifists make different kinds of responses. Some advocate a style of nonresistance. Some would attempt to deal with the attacker in a calm spirit of reason and prayer. Others would defend their families physically to the point of eliminating the attacker if necessary. Some of these would do everything short of actually killing the adversary. Some pacifists would participate in police action but not in war. Others would not participate in police action themselves but would grant its legitimacy for the state in an evil world. Thus we have seen that a pacifist stance against participation in war is held by a wide variety of people whose beliefs about their personal responses to force vary. For myself, I would hope to be faithful to a more absolute position, refusing ever to take the life of another. I cannot assert dogmatically what I would do in any given situation. I hope that God's grace would cause me to obey the way of the life-giving cross above my desire for my own self preservation.

Hypothetical questions may also be an escape from the real questions. Instead of dreaming up or responding to hypothetical questions, we need to be discussing the real ones. Is it right to destroy villages in order to save them? Should millions of men be trained to hate and kill? Can we in any way justify the continual production of nuclear bombs? With hypothetical *and* real questions, however, there is a danger that we may get so hung up discussing them that we forget to ask the really real question for the Christian: "What does it mean to be a disciple of Christ in our kind of world?"

Appendix I

Peace Statements from the Church of the Brethren

A Statement of the Church of the Brethren on War

This statement was originally adopted by the 1948 Annual Conference as the "Statement On Position And Practices Of The Church Of The Brethren In Relation To War." A first revision was made in 1957, a second in 1968. It appears here as revised for the third time by the 1970 Annual Conference.

The Church of the Brethren regards with sorrow and deep concern our nation's increasing movement toward a permanently militaristic outlook. Two devastating world wars, the conflict in Korea, the Vietnam War, and the many international crises of recent decades have produced an alarming change in American attitudes toward war and peace. The American public may come to accept as normal and inevitable the prospect that the nation must be prepared to go to war at any moment, that every young man must spend time in military service, that an overwhelming share of our heavy federal taxes must be devoted to military needs, and that this country must always be willing to assume the military burdens of weaker allies, actual or potential.

Because of our complete dissent from these assumptions, the Church of the Brethren desires again, as at other times in its history, to declare its convictions about war and peace, military service and conscription, the use of tax money for military purposes, the right of Christian conscience, and the responsibility of Christian citizenship.

I. The Church and Spiritual Nurture

The Church of the Brethren seeks by processes of education and spiritual nurture to help its members to allow a spirit of

peace and an attitude of nonviolence to develop within themselves as an outgrowth of deep religious conviction. They are
encouraged to demonstrate this spirit in their daily relationships
in the home, the school, business, and the community.

For this purpose, we provide our services of worship, our
preaching ministry, our Sunday and weekday educational efforts,
our summer camps, our colleges and seminary, our personal
counseling, our volunteer service program, our continuing ministry in relief and rehabilitation, and our entire church-extension
program. We seek thereby to lead individuals into such intimate
contact with Jesus Christ, our Lord, that they will commit themselves to him and to the manner of life which he taught and
exemplified.

We believe that such commitment leads to the way of love and
of nonviolence as a central principle of Christian conduct, knowing full well that, in so doing, violence may fall upon us as it did
upon Jesus. We recognize that there are varying degrees of
achievement of this sought-for result in individuals and
churches. But, we seek to maintain a deep and growing fellowship among ourselves and between ourselves and our Master in
order that we might increasingly know his purpose and do his
will.

II. The Church and Conscience

The church has stood likewise for the principle of freedom of
worship and freedom of conscience. The church itself respects
the right of the individual conscience within its membership and
has never set up an authoritative creed. Instead, it accepts the
entire New Testament as its rule of faith and practice and seeks
to lead its members to comprehend and accept for themselves the
mind of Christ as the guide for their convictions and conduct.

We believe that no government has the authority to abrogate
the right of individual conscience. *"We must obey God rather
than men"* Acts 5:29).

The official position of the Church of the Brethren is that all
war is sin and that we seek the right of conscientious objection to

all war. We seek no special privileges from our government. What we seek for ourselves, we seek for all—the right of individual conscience. We affirm that this conscientious objection may be based on grounds more inclusive than institutional religion.

III. The Church and War

The Church of the Brethren, since its beginning in 1708, has repeatedly declared its position against war. Our understanding of the life and the teaching of Christ, as revealed in the New Testament, led our Annual Conference to state in 1785 that we should not *"submit to the higher powers so as to make ourselves their instruments to shed human blood."* In 1918, at our Annual Conference, we stated that *"we believe that war or any participation in war is wrong and incompatible with the spirit, example, and teachings of Jesus Christ."* Again in 1934, Annual Conference resolved that *"all war is sin. We, therefore, cannot encourage, engage in, or willingly profit from armed conflict at home, or abroad. We cannot, in the event of war, accept military service or support the military machine in any capacity."* This conviction, which we reaffirmed in 1948 and now affirm again, grew out of such teachings of Christ as the following:

> *"Love your enemies, do good to those who hate you, bless those who curse you, pray for those who abuse you. To him who strikes you on the cheek, offer the other also. . ."* (Luke 6:27, 28).

> *"So whatever you wish that men would do to you, do so to them; for this is the law and the prophets"* (Matthew 7:12).

> *"Put your sword back into its place; for all who take the sword will perish by the sword"* (Matthew 26:52).

IV. The Church and Conscription

The Church of the Brethren feels constrained by Christ's teachings to lead its people to develop convictions against war. The church cannot concede to the state the authority to conscript citizens for military training or military service against their conscience.

The church will seek to fulfill its prophet role in this matter in two ways: by seeking to change political structures and by influencing individual members.

The church will seek to use its influence to abolish or radically restructure the system which conscripts persons for military purposes.

The church pledges its support and continuing fellowship to all of our draft-age members who face conscription. We recognize that some feel obligated to render full or noncombative military service and we respect all who make such a decision.

We commend to all of draft age, their parents, counselors and fellow members, the alternative positions of (1) Alternative Service as conscientious objectors engaging in constructive civilian work, or (2) open, nonviolent noncooperation with the system of conscription. The church pledges itself to renew and redouble its efforts to interpret to the membership of the church, at all levels of the church's life, these positions which we believe are in harmony with the style of life set forth in the Gospel and as expressed in the historic faith and witness of our church.

The church extends its prayers, spiritual nurture and material aid to all who struggle and suffer, in order, to understand more fully and obey more perfectly the will of God.

V. The Church and Alternative Service

The church pledges its support to the draft-age member facing conscription who chooses to engage in constructive alternative service civilian work as a conscientious objector. Such service might include participation in relief and rehabilitation in war or disaster areas anywhere in the world; technical, agricultural, medical, or educational assistance in developing countries; service in general or mental hospitals, schools for the handicapped, homes for the aged, and kindred institutions; and medical or scientific research promising constructive benefits to mankind.

The church will seek to establish, administer, and finance to the extent of its resources, projects for such service under church direction or in cooperation with other private civilian agencies.

VI. The Church and Noncooperation

The church pledges its support to the draft-age member facing conscription who chooses open noncooperation with the system of conscription as a conscientious objector. Individuals who follow the lead of their conscience to this position will need the support of the church in many ways. The church will seek to meet these needs, to the extent of its resources, by providing such ministries as legal counsel, financial support, and prison visitation. To demonstrate a sense of community and fellowship with the noncooperator, congregations are encouraged to offer sanctuary and spiritual support. All members of the church who take the position of noncooperation should seek to exhibit a spirit of humility, good-will, and sincerity in making this type of courageous witness most effective, nonviolent, and Christian.

VII. The Church and Ministerial Exemption

The Church of the Brethren accepts the concept of the minister as one who seeks no special privilege, but shares the life of his people. Therefore, the church urges those who have the possibility of ministerial exemption from the draft law to consider refusing such exemption and to confront the draft on an equal basis with the laity.

VIII. The Church and Support of National Defense

We declare, again, that our members should not participate in war, learn the art of war, or support war. Although recognizing that almost all aspects of the economy are directly or indirectly connected with national defense, we encourage our members to divorce themselves, as far as possible, from direct association with defense industries in both employment and investment.

While recognizing the necessity of preserving academic freedom, we find recruitment by the armed forces on Brethren college campuses inconsistent with the church's position.

IX. The Church and Taxes for War Purposes

While the Church of the Brethren recognizes the responsibility of all citizens to pay taxes for the constructive purposes of government, we oppose the use of taxes by the government for war purposes and military expenditures. For those who are conscientiously opposed to paying taxes for these purposes, the church seeks government provision for an alternative use of such tax money for peaceful, nonmilitary purposes.

The church recognizes that its members will believe and act differently in regard to their payment of taxes when a significant percentage goes for war purposes and military expenditures. Some will pay the taxes willingly; some will pay the taxes, but express a protest to the government; some will refuse to pay all or part of the taxes as a witness and a protest; and some will voluntarily limit their incomes or use of taxable services to a low enough level that they are not subject to taxation.

We call upon all of our members, congregations, institutions, and boards, to study seriously the problem of paying taxes for war purposes and investing in those government bonds which support the war. We further call upon them to act in response to their study, to the leading of conscience and to their understanding of the Christian faith. To all we pledge to maintain our continuing ministry of fellowship and spiritual concern.

X. The Church and Citizenship

The church holds that our supreme citizenship is in the kingdom of God, but we undertake to render constructive, creative service in the existing state. We encourage our members to exercise the right of suffrage and to regard public office as an opportunity to work for good government in keeping with our Christian values. We believe that in a democracy, Christians must assume responsibility for helping to create intelligent public opinion which will result in legislation in harmony with the eternal laws of God.

As Christian citizens, we consider it our duty to obey all civil laws which do not violate these higher laws. We seek, however, to go beyond the demands of law, giving time, effort, life, and property in a ministry to human needs without regard to race, creed, or nationality. We attempt to reconcile conflicting persons and groups, leading them toward fuller human brotherhood under a common divine allegiance.

We believe that good citizenship extends beyond our own national boundaries and will there serve to remove the occasions of war. Convinced that good citizens in a good society must work out a better way than war to resolve international conflict, we have in recent years undertaken a diligent search for practical, effective means to that end.

The church encourages its members to study international relations and foreign policy and to confer with legislators, government executives, and other policy makers concerning these matters in the light of the Christian faith. We favor the strengthening of agencies of international cooperation; intelligent sympathy with the desire of the people in underdeveloped areas for self-determination and a higher standard of living; and intensified study and application of the peaceful, constructive uses of atomic power for the benefit of all mankind.

XI. The Church and Its Continuing Witness

The Church of the Brethren has always believed that peace is the will of God. In the two and one half centuries of its history, it has come to understand more clearly the tremendous evil which war brings upon human beings and their society. The church, therefore, feels an increasing responsibility for the careful instruction and guidance of its members on all the problems of war and peace. It is also aware that there is room for further growth in the understanding of these questions and in ways of expressing the church's convictions in practical action.

This statement embodies the stage of thought and action which the Church of the Brethren has thus far reached in its desire to learn the will of God for our times. We undertake a continuing and growing witness and pledge ourselves to be receptive to new truth and better modes of expression as these come to our attention.

Obedience to God and Civil Disobedience

This statement was accepted "as a position paper for the Church of the Brethren" by a two-thirds majority of the 1969 Annual Conference held at Louisville, Kentucky.

Christians have always faced choices which test the relationships between faithfulness to God and responsibility to the state. Today such choices confront us:

How shall we relate to laws which enforce or support racial discrimination, laws which deny welfare aid to some groups of poor people, laws which conscript youth for military and civilian service, laws which require payment of taxes for war purposes, laws which forbid providing food and medical aid to so-called "enemy nations"?

When should we obey God rather than man (Acts 5:29) or refuse to render to Caesar what we consider to be God's (Mark 12:17)? Recently the Church of the Brethren answered this question briefly saying, "When he (a Christian) is profoundly convinced that God forbids what the state demands, it is his responsibility to express his convictions. Such expression may include disobedience of the state" (*Church, State, and Christian Citizenship*, Annual Conference, 1967). A fuller discussion is now needed.

Obedience to God Comes First

Christian faithfulness means obedience to God. The state and its citizens, the church and its members, all are under God and ultimately accountable to him as Creator, Sustainer, Judge, and Redeemer. The sovereignty of the state is limited by the sovereignty of God. While the state may demand reasonable loyalty from its citizens, it must not demand absolute obedience which belongs to God. The state is caught in strong tendencies to act as if it were absolute. We live in a world atmosphere pervaded by nationalisms which snare Christians also into absolutizing their particular country. To the extent that the state does not set itself up as absolute, to the extent that it provides and protects freedom of conscience, and upholds, sustains and promotes just and moral laws, there is no need for citizens to disobey the state in order to obey God. Obedience to civil authority can be consonant then with Christian faithfulness.

The church submits itself to the disciplines of searching the scriptures in openness to the "mind of Christ," to the counsel of the concerned brother, and to prayer. These disciplines may point up a conflict between the demands of the state and God's intentions. In any forced option between loyalty to God and loyalty to the state, the choice for Christians is clear. Obedience to God is their first and highest responsibility, their supreme loyalty, their positive beginning point, their plumb line for decision-making. It is a case of positive obedience to God, though the state may negatively call it "civil disobedience." From the Christian perspective, it is the state which is in the condition of disobedience to God and his purposes for the world.

Jesus, in doing his Father's will, found himself in conflict with the authorities of his day. He deliberately disobeyed Jewish law as he associated with Samaritans and Gentiles. He cleansed the temple of robbing money changers whose presence was protected by law. Central among the accusations which resulted in his crucifixion was the charge of treason. At the same time he consistently avoided the use of violence as a means for bringing in the Messianic kingdom.

Reactive and Initiatory Disobedience

Civil disobedience may be reactive or initiatory. The former occurs when the state demands action which the church or its members cannot do for reasons of conscience and higher loyalty to God. They respond by refusing to obey. Examples of such reactive civil disobedience are refusal to obey laws requiring racial discrimination, noncompliance when conscripted to national service, and nonpayment of taxes for war purposes.

Initiatory civil disobedience may occur when action is initiated to serve human need in a way that happens to transgress laws which themselves support and inflict unjust suffering. Examples of initiatory civil disobedience are the sending of food and medical aid to the suffering civilians in a country with whom our nation is at war, and providing welfare assistance to some groups of poor people when the law denies help for such groups.

The historic Brethren position has tended toward the reactive form of civil disobedience, refusing to submit to those demands of the state to which Brethren have conscientiously objected. Today the church and many of its members are engaging in direct actions that challenge and seek to correct legal injustice. Insofar as these actions, including initiatory civil disobedience, aim toward making government a more effective instrument of righteousness, they should be seen as forms of high patriotism and service to government.

The Record in History

Church history is replete with examples of those who found themselves in conflict with the authorities in the course of expressing their loyalty to God: Peter, Paul, and the early disciples who met together in violation of Roman law, who went to jail because of their ministry, who "turned the world upside down"; the Christians who refused to serve in the Roman army and to pay taxes to Caesar's pagan temples; Martin Luther; the early Anabaptist churches; the founders of the Church of the Brethren; Christians in Hitler's Germany; Dr. Martin Luther

King, Jr. There are many honorable examples in the history of the United States: Quakers who refused to pay taxes for war against the Indians; Henry David Thoreau; Ralph Waldo Emerson; abolitionists who broke the Fugitive Slave Law; citizens and churches who refused to obey laws supporting racial or religious discrimination; persons who send medical aid to North Vietnam in violation of the "trading with the enemy act"; men who return or destroy their draft cards in order to call into question laws they consider unjust, immoral, or unconstitutional.

The Brethren Record

Notable actions can be cited from our Church of the Brethren tradition in America which at the time were considered acts of civil disobediences: refusal to go to the mustering grounds and to pay war taxes during the Revolutionary War; Christopher Sauer II; those who avoided participation in the Civil War; deliberate violations of the Fugitive Slave Law; Elder John Kline; the special Annual Conference, January 9, 1918, at Goshen, Indiana, which advised against wearing the military uniform and performing combatant service. (This statement was declared treasonable by the state and withdrawn by the church.)

Some Policy Questions

Several questions of policy tend to arise when a group considers engaging in civil disobedience in its efforts to be faithful to God.

How large a majority vote should a group have before engaging in such acts?

What protection should be afforded the minority which does not approve or desire to participate in civil disobedience?

What are the rights, freedoms, and responsibilities of the majority and the minority themselves and toward each other?

Where in a large body like the church should responsibility be placed for decisions to engage in civil disobedience?

Upon whom does the law place responsibility for acts of civil disobedience by the church?

How can the church engage in prophetic witness to the state including civil disobedience when a significant number of its members will not support such a witness?

How can the church simultaneously provide for freedom of conscience, democratic decision-making, and prophetic public witness?

Order and Freedom in the Church

The implications of civil disobedience are seldom clear or easily defined for the church. On the one hand, the church possesses the characteristics of any large bureaucratic institution with a well-defined polity, a system of decision-making, and stated relationships between larger and subordinate groups. On the other hand, the church is a voluntary association of committed Christians who have freely joined together for nurture and witness to their discipleship. Since the church is both an institution and a community of believers, there is an inherent tension between order and freedom, between clear-cut procedures and freedom of the spirit, between responsible representative government and the dictates of conscience in individuals and groups.

Any elected body such as a board of directors, the General Board, a district board, a church board, or a commission has responsibilities and roles in at least two directions. First, it is responsible to those who elected it or its constituency. A part of this responsibility is to represent adequately its electorate and to reflect the electorate's views. An elected body is expected to follow the expressed wishes of those who elected it and to sense their "mind and mood." Second, it is expected to develop and maintain its own inner integrity. A part of this responsibility is to follow its own conscience, its own best insights. It is expected to lead its constituency, not merely to follow; to serve a prophetic role as well as a priestly one.

The formation of action or covenantal groups within the institutional church provides an additional way of maintaining creativity, openness, and prophetic witness in the church. The church should permit and encourage those who are prepared to take a united stand on basic social issues of our day. They should be offered a ministry of love, concern, fellowship, counsel, and any needed material care.

When a minority group takes a position different from majority opinion or commits an act of civil disobedience that has not received approval by the larger body, the group should indicate carefully that it is acting on its own and representing only itself.

Placement of Responsibility

Where is responsibility to be placed when individuals, action groups, or representative corporate church bodies commit acts of civil disobedience in their efforts to be faithful to God? The placement of responsibility for such acts is clearest when they are committed by individuals representing only themselves. Responsibility for such actions by small covenant groups is usually placed upon the members because each has voluntarily assented to participation, even though the group has acted corporately or unitedly.

Most representative or corporate church bodies become legally incorporated and elect a board of directors to represent and serve them as their "legal corporation." The General Board is the legal corporation for the Church of the Brethren, the district board for the district, and the church board for the congregation. When a church body does not legally incorporate with a board of directors, the law generally holds its officers or leaders responsible for any illegal activity or civil disobedience.

The board of directors of any corporation carries responsibility for assessing the "mind" of the organization's full membership, and for planning, deciding, executing, and bearing the consequences related to any act of civil disobedience which it commits on behalf of the organization. The law holds all members of a board of directors responsible for such a violation of law except those board members who explicitly asked to be recorded as voting against the action. The nondirector members of an incorporated body are not held legally responsible for any act of civil disobedience committed by the board of directors unless they have formally ratified or approved the board's action.

A court may assess fines against a corporation as a "legal individual" and/or against individual members of its board of directors. All members of the board of directors who vote for or participate in the action are subject to any imprisonment penalties stipulated in the law.

Criminal law is more concerned with the manner of an act than with its motive. It is more concerned with a violator's intent, deliberateness, and willfulness than with his motive, purpose, or goal. One who willfully violates a law in the act of obeying God is judged more severely in the courts than one who violates the law accidentally, unintentionally, unknowingly. In order for a court to convict one of a violation of criminal law, it must prove that the law was violated *both by intent and by an act*.

Some Guidelines for Action

Christians are called to obey whatever the cost. Christian faithfulness may bring on or require civil disobedience. This is a serious and drastic step which should be thought through carefully, prayed about, and fully discussed. Its legal and other consequences should be understood, and the state's authority to punish law violators recognized.

Christians should appreciate and support the worthy functions which government performs and willingly obey the state in matters on which they have no contrary moral convictions. Indeed, Christians should see the state as an instrument for serving God and help to make and mold it into a more fitting instrument. Civil disobedience usually should be considered only after all legal means to correct injustice have failed.

Christians should be encouraged to put into writing those goals which may precipitate civil disobedience in order that their purposes are clear, can be examined, and can be communicated accurately to others. Such statements also may describe their previous efforts toward changing the law through the normal procedures of government, and their intention to continue such efforts.

The emphasis of the action should be upon faithfulness to God and the affirmation of clear moral issues rather than upon the negation of law and civil disobedience as an end in itself.

Dialogue with civil authorities regarding plans should normally precede and continue during acts of civil disobedience.

Christians should always adhere to nonviolence, avoiding harm and minimizing inconvenience to others. At the same time they should prepare for the consequences of any civil disobedience which may grow out of their obedience to God. Suffering may be the price of their active witness; but suffering for Christ is counted a blessing.

In corporate church bodies the decision to engage in civil disobedience should be based on a substantial majority vote, such as two-thirds. When a minority remains unconvinced, the majority should consider all the more carefully whether the contemplated civil disobedience is something it must in obedience proceed with, even apart from the minority. Those within the corporate body who do not agree with the majority decision to engage in civil disobedience should not only the right to vote "no" but to have their names recorded for the legal record if they request it, to have their minority viewpoint respected, and to receive the love, concern and fellowship of the majority. The officers, the board of directors, and the members in any corporate body voting to participate in civil disobedience should recognize the possible consequences of their action, thus "counting the cost."

A Concluding Word

If we believe that God has one will for his people, a Christian fellowship should search diligently and prayerfully for that will. It should strive toward "one mind" and a common obedience even if that means a common civil disobedience. On many issues in relation to the law and the state a Christian fellowship will be able to come to "one mind." On some issues, however, conscientious Christians will differ in their understanding of what it means to obey God. Some will accept or support a particular law while others will disobey it or revolt against the state.

In such controversial situations members of the church should respect and appreciate the sincerity and commitment of those who differ in their understanding of the kind of action called for by obedience to God. Members should endeavor to "listen" and to "hear" one another in a continuing brotherly encounter as to what constitutes obedience. Whether they are in the majority or the minority on any question, Christians should avoid being self-righteous, judgmental, or resentful toward any who do not take their position. In mature Christian fellowship members love and respect one another even when, in seeking to obey God, some deliberately disobey a law while others support it.

Above all, Christian persons and groups are called to be obedient and faithful to Christ's will and way. Even though such obedience brings them into conflict with a law and the state, their first and highest obedience is to God.

Appendix II

Peace Statements from the Mennonite Churches

A MESSAGE FROM THE INTERNATIONAL MENNONITE PEACE COMMITTEE

Mennonite World Conference, XI Assembly
Strasbourg, July 24 to 29, 1984

Introduction

This is a brief message from the Peace Committee related to the Mennonite World Conference. We address these words to local Mennonite and Brethren in Christ congregations around the world. We share our analysis and our vision, and invite your counsel. **We invite you to use this statement as a basis for study and action.**

The human family faces staggering problems of malnutrition, hunger, disease and war. Political and economic powers exploit the human and natural resources of the earth for their own selfish purposes. We in our local churches may not be sure how to respond to these problems, but let us decide to live in solidarity with one another under God. Some of us live under systems that exploit others. Some of us suffer heavy burdens because others exploit us. We are linked with one another. It is appropriate, therefore, that we should ask in our local congregations: "What is the message of the Gospel for these times?"

We believe that the same Jesus who redeems us is also our peace and our security. The life of Jesus and the message of the Scriptures guide us in our witness to the way of peace and justice. (See the Prophetic writings of the Old Testament: Ephesians 1 to 3; Colossians 2:15; Matthew 5 to 7.)

The Role of the Church in the Nation

What is the role of the church in society and among the nations? God has ordained government to order the affairs of society. But God is sovereign and all governments are subject to the authority of God. The church, as part of the Kingdom of God, witnesses to the will of God for society even if the state is disobedient to the intention of God. There is no place for imposing the will of God on government. But the task of the church is to create expectations for peace and justice as she witnesses to the Lord of the Kingdom of God. If the church is silent how shall the nations know if they are unfaithful to God's mandate? As Takio Tanase of Japan said in our midst, I Peter and other Scripture passages direct governments to "punish those who do wrong and praise those who do right." The crisis in our time is that some governments persecute those who do right—those who seek freedom to worship and to practice their faith; some governments punish citizens who speak against the ways of violence and oppression.

Hunger and the Arms Race

Nations of the earth now rely on military means to stay in power and to solve national and international conflict. They sacrifice the security and the good of their own people so they have money to buy weapons. Eleven million babies die every year before their first birthday because of malnutrition and disease. Thirty children of the world die every minute because of hunger and sickness. And every minute governments spend 1.3 million dollars for military purposes. The judgement of Isaiah 1:16-17 and Isaiah 10:1-2 speaks to our times:

> *Wash yourselves; make yourselves clean; remove the evil of your doings from before my eyes; cease to do evil; learn to do good; seek justice, correct oppression; defend the fatherless, plead for the widow . . . defend the rights of the needy.*

Surely God's people must call leaders of the world to account for this wicked injustice.

The Threat of Nuclear War

The threat of nuclear war and the potential nuclear pollution of the environment have been described as the chief moral issues of our time. Nuclear weapons not only kill; they destroy all life. As God's people we serve in hope even in the face of the nuclear threat. So we do not despair. Rather, we witness courageously to the Lord of all creation.

Conclusion

Our Committee believes that this message is rooted in the evangelistic and ethical vocation of the church. We confess that we need the reconciling work of God in our local congregations. But let us also join other Christians of East and West, North and South in proclaiming the word of life in a world of death. Let this sure word go forth through our churches to "all nations, for all authority has been given to Jesus who will be with us to the end of the age" (Matthew 28:19-20).

A Declaration of Christian faith and commitment . . .

Adopted at a Study Conference on Nonresistance held by Representatives of the Mennonite and Brethren in Christ Churches of North America at Winona Lake, Indiana, November 9-12, 1950

I

At this mid-point of the 20th century, at a critical time in a generation marked by wide-spread and disastrous wars and shadowed by the threat of still more ruinous warfare, this conference of delegated representatives from the Mennonite and Brethren in Christ churches of the United States and Canada unites in a renewed declaration of faith in Jesus Christ, the Prince of Peace, in His Gospel, and in His power to redeem and transform in life and in human society all those who receive Him as Saviour and Lord and are thus born anew by the Spirit of God. It also unites in a deeper commitment to follow Christ in full discipleship in the way of peace and love, the way of nonresistance and peacemaking. In this conference we have seen anew the high calling of the sons of God, having been confronted with the absolute claims which Christ makes upon us. We acknowledge these claims in full, and have sought to trace the meaning of His Lordship and the consequences of our commitment in earnest and informed conversation together and in urgent prayer to God for grace and light, seeking to know His will for us in this day.

In our common consideration we have come to certain united convictions expressed in the following declarations which we now humbly send as our message to all our churches both in America and throughout the world as well as to all others who own Christ as Lord. To our brethren we say, this is the day for us to take a clear and unwavering stand on the great essentials of the Gospel and Christian discipleship. It is a day in which to demonstrate and proclaim courageously and unflinchingly this redemptive Gospel and this life of love and service in its fullness and its glory. Let us do so in united purpose with one heart and voice, trusting in the power of God and the companionship of our Lord who has promised to be with us alway.

II

1. It is our faith that one is our Master, even Christ, to whom alone supreme loyalty and obedience is due, who is our only Saviour and Lord.

2. It is our faith that by the renewing grace of God which makes us new creatures in Christ, and alone thereby, we can through the power of the indwelling Spirit live the life of holy obedience and discipleship to which all the sons of God are called, for His grace does forgive and heal the penitent sinner and brings us to a new life of fellowship with Him and with one another.

3. It is our faith that redeeming love is at the heart of the Gospel, coming from God and into us to constrain us to love Him and our neighbor, and that such love must henceforth be at the center of every thought and act.

4. It is our faith that Christ has established in His church a universal community and brotherhood within which the fullness of Christ's reign must be practiced, into which the redeemed must be brought, and from which must go out into all human society the saving and healing ministry of the Gospel.

5. It is our faith that the life of love and peace is God's plan for the individual and the race, and that therefore discipleship means the abandonment of hatred, strife and violence in all human relations, both individual and social.

III

These declarations of faith give no blueprint for peace nor do they assume that human endeavor alone can bring about a warless world within history, for only when men come under the Lordship of Christ can they make peace and fulfill the prayer of our Lord, "Thy Kingdom come, Thy will be done on earth as in heaven." They do, however, require certain attitudes, duties and ministries of us, to which we do here by God's grace declare our adherence and our determination to undertake in His name.

1. Our love and ministry must go out to all men regardless of race or condition, within or without the brotherhood, whether friend or foe, and must seek to bring the Gospel and all its benefits to every one. Race or class prejudice must never be found among us.

2. We do recognize fully that God has set the state in its place of power and ministry. But, recognizing the relative and condi-

tional validity of any particular form of government and of concrete legislative, executive and judicial acts, we hold that we
must judge all things in the light of God's Word and see that our
responses to the relativities of the state and its workings are
always conformed to the absolutes of Christian discipleship and
love. We acknowledge our obligation to witness to the powers
that be of the righteousness which God requires of all men, even
in government, and beyond this to continue in earnest interces-
sion to God on their behalf.

3. We do have the responsibility to bring to the total social
order of which we are a part, and from which we receive so
much, the utmost of which we are capable in Christian love and
service. Seeking for all men first the kingdom of God and His
righteousness, we must hold together in one united ministry the
evangelism which brings men to Christ and the creative application of the Gospel to cultural, social and material need; for we
find that the true and ultimate goal of evangelism is the Chris-
tianization of the whole of life and the creation of the fully
Christian community within the fellowship of faith. For this reason the social order, including our own segment of it, must be
constantly brought under the judgment of Christ.

4. We cannot be satisfied to retain for ourselves and our communities alone, in any kind of self-centered and isolated enjoy-
ment, the great spiritual and material goods which God has
bestowed upon us, but are bound in loving outreach to all to bear
witness and to serve, summoning men everywhere to the life of
full discipleship and to the pursuit of peace and love without
limit. Separately and together we must use every feasible way
and facility for this ministry: the spoken and written word; the
demonstration of holiness and love in family, church, and community; relief work and social service; and all other ways. We
must enlist many more of our people in such witness and
service, both as a major purpose of their life and for specific
projects and terms. Especially now must Christian love and
redemptive action find expression in our ministry of service,
when men are turning more and more to the use of force and war
in futile attempts to solve the urgent problems of our world. In

this service our youth can play a great part. They should give themselves to it in large numbers, both for shorter terms and in lifetime dedication.

5. Parallel with this we must practice an increasingly sharper Christian control of our economic, social and cultural practices among ourselves and toward others, to make certain that love truly operates to work no ill to our neighbor, either short-range or long-range. Knowing how much the selfishness, pride and greed of individuals, groups, and nations, which economic systems often encourage, help to cause carnal strife and warfare, we must see to it that we do not contribute thereto, whether for the goals of direct military operations or to anything which destroys property or causes hurt or loss of human life.

6. While rejecting any social system or ideology such as atheistic communism, which opposes the Gospel and would destroy the true Christian faith and way of life, we cannot take any attitude or commit any act contrary to Christian love against those who hold or promote such views or practices, but must seek to overcome their evil and win them through the Gospel.

7. We cannot compromise with war in any form. In case of renewed compulsion by the state in any form of conscription of service or labor, money or goods, including industrial plants, we must find ways to serve our countries and the needs of men elsewhere, in ways which will give significant and necessary benefits, which will keep our Christian testimony uncompromised, particularly with respect to war, and which will make possible a faithful representation of Christ and His love. We cannot therefore participate in military service in any form. We cannot have any part in financing war operations or preparations through war bonds. We cannot knowingly participate in the manufacture of munitions, weapons, and instruments of war or destruction. We cannot take part in scientific, educational, or cultural programs designed to contribute to war, or in any propaganda or activity that tends to promote ill-will or hatred among men or nations. We must rather foster good will, understanding, and mutual regard and help among all nations, races, and classes. And we cannot as churches lend ourselves to the direct

administration of conscription or state compulsion, seeking rather to find voluntary patterns of service through which the demands of the state may be both satisfied and transcended, and going with our men in whatever civilian service they give.

8. If war does come with its possible serious devastation from bombings or other forms of destruction, such as atomic blasts, germ warfare, poison gas, etc., we will willingly render every help which conscience permits, sacrificially and without thought of personal safety, so long as we thereby help to preserve and restore life and not to destroy it.

IV

While we are deeply grateful to God for the precious heritage of faith including the principle of love and nonresistance,* which our Swiss, Dutch, and German Anabaptist-Mennonite forefathers purchased for us by their faith, obedience, and sacrifice, and which we believe is again expressed in the above declarations and commitments, we are convinced that this faith must be repossessed personally by each one out of his own reading and obeying of God's Word, and must ever be spelled out in life practice anew. Hence, we summon our brotherhood to a deeper mastery of the Scriptures as the infallible revelation of God's will for us, and to a finding afresh under Holy Spirit guidance of its total message regarding Christ's way and its application in our present world.

We humbly confess our inadequacies and failures both in understanding and in following this way, knowing well that we have come short both in demonstration and proclamation of Christian love. As we renew our commitment of discipleship and ambassadorship for Christ, we know how much we need God's grace and each other's help in the fellowship of His body in learning and obeying. Let us therefore stand together and go on together in His name and for His cause.

---

*A faith universally held by the Mennonites of all lands for the first three centuries of our history and continuously confessed by all groups in North America until this day.

Appendix III

Peace Statements from the Society of Friends

George Fox, 1651

I told [the Commonwealth Commissioners] I lived in the virtue of that life and power that took away the occasion of all wars and I knew from whence all wars did rise, from the lust, according to James's doctrine . . . I told them I was come into the covenant of peace which was before wars and strifes were.

Declaration to Charles II, 1661

We utterly deny all outward wars and strife and fightings with outward weapons, for any end or under any pretence whatsoever. And this is our testimony to the whole world. The spirit of Christ, by which we are guided, is not changeable, so as once to command us from a thing as evil and again to move unto it; and we do certainly know, and so testify to the world, that the spirit of Christ, which leads us into all Truth, will never move us to fight and war against any man with outward weapons, neither for the kingdom of Christ, nor for the kingdoms of this world.

Yearly Meeting, 1912, 1925

We are deeply convinced that the testimony for Peace, which we believe has been entrusted to us as a Society, is not an artificial appendage to our faith, which can be dropped without injuring the whole, but rather an organic out-growth of our belief as Christians and as Friends, which cannot be abandoned without mutilating our whole message for the world.

We believe in common with other Christians, that in Jesus Christ, the Divine Word, which in all ages had been the 'Light' of men, took human form. We have seen in him the revelation of the priceless worth of manhood in the sight of God, and know that in virtue of his 'Light' shed abroad in every human soul, all men, of whatever race or nation, are brothers. Upon this sacred human personality, war rudely tramples, virtually regarding men as *things*, as obstacles to be got rid of, if they are enemies; or, if they are our own soldiers, as military instruments whose consciences may be disregarded. As Christians we cannot be parties to putting ourselves or others in such a position. Further, since the Divine Light within us is the Light of Christ, we cannot separate it from the spirit of his teaching, when he was here on earth. We cannot claim his authority for impulses within us which lead us to act in opposition to that teaching, which he summed up in love to God and love to all men.

In so far as we have grasped and been obedient to these leadings, we have been enabled to see a splendid vision of what human unity is, and of what human fellowship may be, and have of necessity been filled with a profound sense of the evil of violating this fellowship. This vision has brought us a renewed faith in the power of spiritual forces to build the structure of humanity, and to redeem it from error and wrong. It is only spiritual forces that can do this, the powers that touch men's hearts, that convince their minds and win their loyalty and set free the uniting forces of humanity. The very refusal of all violence, if it springs evidently and sincerely from a deep reverence and love for 'that of God' in an opponent's nature, will be potent to reach and win his soul. Those who see this, even if dimly and amid much perplexity, must hold it fast.

We have so valued this vision and recognised its authority that war—'the arbitrament of self-assertion and passion', with all its abrogation of moral restraint, its denial of discriminating justice, its responsibility for atrocities, its destruction of all the divine possibilities of human life—is for us an impossibility.

Backed by these convictions, we hold the moral law of gentleness and forgiveness and love to be unconditionally binding upon us now. It seems a poor and pitiful thing to believe in principles except when they may have to be applied, in forgiveness only when there is nothing to forgive, in love only for those who love us. It is our present sinning and stricken world that needs these redeeming messages in word and life. May we be faithful to the vision! It bears with it a grave but splendid responsibility.

Friends World Conference, 1952

Our peace testimony is much more than our special attitude to world affairs; it expresses our vision of the whole Christian way of life; it is our way of living in this world, of looking at this world and of changing this world. Only when the seeds of war— pride, prestige, and lust for power and possessions—have been purged from our personal and corporate ways of living; only when we can meet all men as friends in a spirit of sharing and caring, can we call upon others to tread the same path.

Our Christian Pacifism, expressed in lives dedicated to the service of God and all his family, should be an experience from which we may speak to peoples and rulers and which transforms a negative refusal to take part in war into a positive witness to the better way. We must by study, by group discussion, and by experience of active peace work equip ourselves with reliable knowledge to enable us not only to expound but also to apply our peace testimony.

---

*The above selections were taken from *Christian faith and practice in the experience of the Society of Friends* (London: London Yearly Meeting, 1960, 1963), Ch. 14, items 605-624.

Endnotes

Chapter 1. A Peace Church and the Peace Churches

1. Otto Piper, *Protestantism in an Ecumenical Age* (Philadelphia: Fortress Press, 1965), pp. 169-170.
2. John Howard Yoder, "The Unique Role of the Historic Peace Churches," a speech given at the Historic Peace Churches Conference, New Windsor, Maryland, Nov. 20, 1968, and published in *Brethren Life and Thought,* 14 (Summer, 1969), p. 144.

Chapter 2. The Pacifist Heritage of the Brethren

1. For a fuller understanding of Anabaptism and the Radical Reformation see Donald Durnbaugh's *The Believers' Church* (New York: Macmillan Company, 1968), ch 3. For treatment of the relationship of Anabaptism to the Brethren see an article by the same author, "Membership in the Body of Christ as Interpreted by the Radical Reformation," *Brethren Life and Thought,* 9 (Autumn, 1964), pp. 50-62.
2. Though similar in meaning and some beliefs, the designations of "Anabaptists" and "New Baptists" should not be confused with the many Baptist groups which stem from English Puritanism of the seventeenth century. The relationship between Anabaptism and English Baptist developments is disputed among scholars.
3. Harry Emerson Fosdick, *Great Voices of the Reformation* (New York: Random House, 1952), p. 291.
4. Donald Durnbaugh, ed., *European Origins of the Brethren* (Elgin, IL: Brethren Press, 1958), p. 343.
5. For a fuller interpretation of Pietism and its importance for the Church of the Brethren see Allen C. Deeter's "Membership in the Body of Christ as Interpreted by Classical Pietism," *Brethren Life and Thought,* 9 (Autumn 1964), pp. 30-49.
6. Samuel Smith, *History of the Province of Pennsylvania.* (Philadelphia: J.B. Lippincott Co., 1913), pp. 188-189.
7. *Ibid.,* p. 180.
8. Translated by Peter Brock, *Pacifism in the United States* (Princeton, NJ: Princeton University Press, 1968), p. 172.
9. Quoted from Rufus Bowman, *The Church of the Brethren and War* (Elgin, IL: Brethren Publishing House, 1944), p. 74.
10. *Ibid.,* p. 75.
11. *Ibid.,* p. 80.
12. *Ibid.,* p. 80.

13. *Minutes of the Annual Meetings of the Church of the Brethren 1778-1909* (Elgin, IL: Brethren Publishing House, 1909), p. 5.
14. *Ibid.*, pp. 6-7.
15. *Ibid.*, p. 7.
16. In the contest of the bicentennial celebration of the United States (1976) peace church historians have added to our understanding of this story through fresh research and stimulating insights. Excellent examples are Donald Durnbaugh, "The Brethren and the Revolution: Neutrals or Tories?" *Brethren Life and Thought*, 22 (Winter, 1977), pp. 13-22; and Richard K. MacMaster with Samuel L. Horst and Robert F. Ulle, *Conscience in Crisis: Mennonites and Other Peace Churches in America, 1739-1789* (Scottdale, PA: Herald Press, 1979).
17. *Minutes of the Annual Meetings,* pp. 9-10.
18. *Ibid.*, p. 48.
19. *Ibid.*, p. 148.
20. *Ibid.*, p. 232.
21. Bowman, *Church of the Brethren and War,* p. 121.
22. Brock, *Pacifism in the United States,* p. 807.
23. Benjamin Funk, *Life of John Kline* (Elgin, IL: Brethren Publishing House, 1900), p. 246.
24. This practice has been confirmed often in conversations I have had with older members of the church. The 1848 Annual Conference Minutes indicated, "The applicant is to declare his agreement with us in regard to the principles of being (nonresistant) non-swearing, and non-conforming to the world." See Henry Kurtz, ed. *The Brethren's Encyclopedia* (Columbiana, OH: for the Editor 1867), p. 38.
25. *The Brethren's Tracts and Pamphlets* (Elgin, IL: Brethren Publishing House, 1900).
26. Bowman, *Church of the Brethren and War,* p. 202.
27. *Ibid.*, p. 181.
28. *Brethren Social Policy* (Elgin, IL. Brethren Press, 1961), p. 44.
29. *Ibid.*
30. *Ibid.*
31. *Annual Conference Minutes, 1911* (Elgin, IL: Brethren Publishing House, printed annually) p. 7.
32. Bowman, *Church of the Brethren and War,* p. 169.
33. *Minutes of the Annual Conference of the Church of the Brethren 1923-1944* (Elgin, IL: Brethren Publishing House, 1944), pp. 110-111.
34. Harry A. Brandt, *The Conquest of Peace* (Elgin, IL: Brethren Publishing House, 1930), inside cover.
35. *Annual Conference Minutes, 1970* (see Appendix I) p. 65.

Chapter 3. Variations Within the Peace Church Tradition

1. *What Does Christ Say About War?* (Scottdale, PA: Herald Press, 1964), p. 3.
2. "Nonresistance and Responsibility," *Concern* (November 1958), p. 24.
3. *Christian Faith and Practice,* London Yearly Meeting, 1960, Section 614.
4. Harry K. Zeller, Jr., "My Hope for Our Future Witness in International Affairs," *Gospel Messenger,* April, 26, 1958, p. 24.
5. *Annual Conference Minutes, 1918,* p. 7.
6. Kenneth L. Brown, "Updating Brethren Values: Rule Pacifism," *Brethren Life and Thought,* 12 (Summer, 1967), p. 23.
7. Duane Friesen, *Mennonite Witness on Peace and Social Concerns: 1900-1980* (Akron, PA: Mennonite Central Committee, 1982), p. 10.
8. *Minutes of the Annual Conference of the Church of the Brethren, 1955-1964* (Elgin, IL: Brethren Press, 1965), p. 77.
9. James Douglass, *The Non-violent Cross* (New York: Macmillan Co., 1966), p. 172.

Chapter 4. Biblical Themes for Peacemaking

1. G. H. C. Macgregor, *The New Testament Basis of Pacifism* (New York: Fellowship Publications, 1936). Though older this is still a valuable exegetical examination of the texts most often used to support and critique pacifism. A newer study is Richard McSorley, *New Testament Basis of Peacemaking* (Scottdale, PA: Herald Press, 1985). Dale Aukerman's *Darkening Valley: A Biblical Perspective on Nuclear War* (New York: Seabury Press, 1981) brings a fresh, creative, and profound exegesis to the nuclear situation and other questions of violence. Many who have milked dry traditional peace texts will discover yet new ones in Aukerman, as well as new insights about familiar ones.
2. Dietrich Bonhoeffer, *Creation and Fall* (New York: Macmillan Co., 1965).
3. Norman Gottwald, *The Tribes of Israel* (Maryknoll, NY: Orbis Books, 1979).
4. Peter C. Craigie, *The Problem of War in the Old Testament* (Grand Rapids, MI: William B. Eerdmans, 1978).
5. Millard C. Lind, *Yahweh Is a Warrior* (Scottdale, PA: Herald Press, 1980.)
6. For an excellent expansion of these themes see Chapter XII, "Christ as Saviour and Pattern," of Vernard Eller's *Kierkegaard and Radical Discipleship* (Princeton, NJ: Princeton University Press, 1968).

7. Dietrich Bonhoeffer, *Ethics* (New York: Macmillan Co., 1961), p. 18.
8. Dietrich Bonhoeffer, *The Cost of Discipleship* (New York: Macmillan Company, 1963), pp. 218-219.
9. For a more complete discussion of this point see Hans-Werner Bartsch's lecture given at Bethany Theological Seminary "The Foundation and Meaning of Christian Pacifism," reprinted in *New Theology No. 6*, ed. by Martin Marty and Dean Peerman (New York: Macmillan Company, 1969), p. 193.

Chapter 5. Hope and the Nuclear Crisis

1. Alan Geyer, Director of the Churches' Center for Theology and Public Policy, Washington, D.C., has written a book which offers reliable data about the arms race to thoughtful Christians. *The Idea of Disarmament*, rev. ed. (Elgin, IL: Brethren Press, 1985). Donald B. Kraybill's *Facing Nuclear War* (Scottdale, PA: Herald Press, 1982) frames both facts and statistics with biblical perspectives in a highly readable style.
2. Merri Wood as quoted in an article, "The Bombmakers," *Chicago Tribune*, August 6, 1985.
3. Stanley Hauerwas, "Surviving Justly: An Ethical Analysis of Nuclear Disarmament," *Religious Conscience and Nuclear Warfare* (Columbia, MO: Univ. of Missouri Press, 1982), p. 7.
4. Aukerman, *Darkening Valley*, p. 130.
5. Quoted by Alan Geyer, "The Pains of Peace at Vancouver," *The Christian Century* (August 31-September 7, 1983), p. 766.
6. (New York: Alfred Knopf, 1982). Some of Schell's ideas were later modified in his *The Abolition* (New York: Alfred Knopf, 1984).
7. Hannah Arendt, *On Violence* (New York: Harcourt, Brace & World, 1970).

Chapter 6. Peace, Justice, and Liberation

1. "Violence, Nonviolence, and the Struggle for Social Justice" (Geneva, Switzerland, August 28, 1973) in Donald F. Durnbaugh, ed., *On Earth Peace* (Elgin: Brethren Press, 1978), pp. 373-385.
2. Lowell H. Zuck, *Christianity and Revolution: Radical Christian Testimonies 1520-1650* (Philadelphia: Temple Univ. Press, 1975).
3. See the excellent discussion of this point in C. Arnold Snyder, *The Relevance of Anabaptist Nonviolence for Nicaragua Today* (Akron, PA: Mennonite Central Committee, Peace Section, 1984), p. 10.

4. There has been growing acceptance of the biblical documentation of this thesis by Mennonite, John Howard Yoder, *The Politics of Jesus* (Grand Rapids, MI: Wm. B. Eerdmans Pub., 1972).
5. John Pairman Brown, *The Liberated Zone* (Richmond, VA: John Knox Press, 1969), p. 87.
6. Snyder, *The Relevance of Anabaptist Nonviolence for Nicaragua Today,* p. 15.
7. *Ibid.,* p. 15. A former professor at Bluffton College, the author of this pamphlet is one who has laid his life on the line. Shortly after delivering this address (1984 C. H. Smith Peace Lecture) he, his wife Linda, and their four children began an eighteen month term in Nicaragua coordinating the activities of "Witness for Peace."

Chapter 7. Disarming the Powers and Principalities

1. Friesen, *Mennonite Witness on Peace and Social Concerns.*
2. John Howard Yoder appropriated the work of H. Berkhof, C. B. Caird, Markus Barth and others in his chapter "Christ and Power," *The Politics of Jesus* (Grand Rapids, MI: Wm. B. Eerdmans, Pub., 1972), pp. 135-162. My thinking is obviously indebted to these interpretations.
3. *Annual Conference Minutes, 1918,* p. 5.
4. Dale Aukerman, *Darkening Valley,* p. 23.
5. This summary statement reflects the Church of the Brethren Annual Conference position paper, "Obedience to God and Civil Disobedience," which is included in the Appendix.
6. Hendrik Berkhof, *Christ and the Powers.* Tr. John H. Yoder (Scottdale, PA: Herald Press, 1977), p. 39.
7. For fuller definition and examples of these terms see H. Richard Niebuhr, *Christ and Culture* (New York: Harper and Row, 1951).
8. Yoder, *Politics of Jesus,* p. 162.

Chapter 8. Shalom Life Styles.

1. Parker Palmer, *Escape and Engagement.* Pendle Hill Bulletin no. 270 (Wallingford, PA, March 1975), p. 7.
2. Most of these themes are explicated in Matthew Fox, *On Becoming a Musical Mystical Bear* (New York: Harper and Row, 1972). More substantive is Fox's recent work *Original Blessing* (Sante Fe, NM: Bear & Co., 1983).
3. See John Howard Yoder's chapter on "Revolutionary Subordination," in his *The Politics of Jesus.*
4. Bonhoeffer, *The Cost of Discipleship,* p. 69.
5. (Elgin, IL: Brethren Press, 1980)

Chapter 9. What If

1. John Howard Yoder, *What Would You Do?* (Scottdale, PA: Herald Press, 1983). This book expands the theological arguments and offers many additional examples of hypothetical situations. It also offers additional concrete examples of cases in which nonviolent responses have been remarkably successful.
2. Joan Baez, "What Would You Do If" from *Daybreak* (New York: Dial Press, 1966), pp. 131-134.
3. Gene Sharp, *The Politics of Nonviolent Action* (Boston: Porter Sargent Publishers, 1973). This massive work is available in three paperbacks entitled *Power and Struggle, The Methods of Nonviolent Action,* and *The Dynamics of Nonviolent Action* from the same publisher, 1974. More peace church activists need to be aware of Sharp's extensive research.

Selected Bibliography

The following books and pamphlets provide a broad perspective
of the peace church witness against war and militarism.

Arnett, Ronald C., *Dwell in Peace: Applying Nonviolence to Everyday
Relationships*. Elgin, IL: Brethren Press, 1980.

Aukerman, Dale, *Darkening Valley: A Biblical Perspective on Nuclear
War*. New York: Seabury, 1980.

Bainton, Roland, *Christian Attitudes Toward War and Peace*. Nash-
ville: Abington Press, 1979.

Berkhof, Hendrick, *Christ and the Powers*. Tr. John Howard Yoder.
Scottdale, PA: Herald Press, 1977.

Bowman, Rufus, *The Church of the Brethren and War*. Elgin, IL:
Brethren Publishing House, 1944.

Brinton, Howard H. *Sources of the Quaker Peace Testimony*. Pendle
Hill Publications, n.d.

Brock, Peter, *Pacifism in the United States from the Colonial Era to the
First World War*. Princeton, NJ: Princeton Univ. Press, 1968.

Brock, Peter, *Twentieth-Century Pacifism*. New York: Van Nostrand
Reinhold, 1970.

Brock, Peter, *Pioneers of the Peacable Kingdom: The Quaker Peace
Testimony from the Colonial Era to the First World War*. Princeton,
NJ: Princeton Univ. Press, 1970.

Brown, Dale W., ed., *What About the Russians?* Elgin, IL: Brethren
Press, 1984.

Clouse, Robert G., *War: Four Christian Views*. Downers Grove, IL:
InterVarsity Press, 1981.

Cochrane, Arthur, *The Mystery of Peace*. Elgin, IL: Brethren Press,
1986.

Craigie, Peter C., *The Problem of War in the Old Testament*. Grand
Rapids, MI: Eerdmans Pub., 1978.

Cronk, Sandra. *Peace Be with You:* A Study of the Spiritual Basis of
the *Friends Peace Testimony*. Philadelphia: Tract Association of
Friends, [c1984].

Durnbaugh, Donald F., *The Believers' Church*. Scottdale, PA: Herald
Press, 1968, 1985.

Durnbaugh, Donald F., ed., *Church of the Brethren Yesterday and
Today*. Elgin, IL: Brethren Press, 1986.

Durnbaugh, Donald F., ed., *On Earth Peace. Discussions on War/ Peace Issues Between Friends, Mennonites, Brethren and European Churches.* Elgin, IL: Brethren Press, 1978.

Durnbaugh, Donald F., ed., *To Serve the Present Age. The Brethren Service Story.* Elgin, IL: Brethren Press, 1975.

Eller, Vernard, *Kierkegaard and Radical Discipleship.* Princeton, NJ: Princeton Univ. Press, 1968.

Eller, Vernard, *War and Peace from Genesis to Revelation.* Scottdale, PA: Herald Press, 1981.

Eisan, Leslie, *Pathways of Peace.* Elgin, IL: Brethren Publishing House, 1948.

Enz, Jacob J., *The Christian and Warfare: The Old Testament, War, and the Christian.* Scottdale, PA: Herald Press, 1972.

Geyer, Alan, *The Idea of Disarmament!* Elgin, IL: Brethren Press, 1985, rev. ed.

Gingerich, Melvin, *Service for Peace. A History of the Mennonite Civilian Public Service.* Akron, PA: Mennonite Central Committee, 1949.

Gottwald, Norman, *The Tribes of Israel.* Marynoll, NY: Orbis Books, 1979.

Hadley, Norval, ed., *New Call to Peacemaking. A Challenge to All Friends.* Philadelphia: Faith and Life Movement, 1976.

Hershberger, Guy F., *War, Peace, and Nonresistance.* Scottdale, PA: Herald Press, 1969, rev. ed.

Hirst, Margret E., *The Quakers in Peace and War.* London: Swarthmore Press, 1923.

Hornus, Jean-Michel, *It Is Not Lawful for Me to Fight.* Scottdale, PA: Herald Press, 1980.

Jones, T. Camby, *The Biblical Basis of Conscientious Objection.* American Friends Service Committee (pamphlet, n.d.)

Jones, T. Camby, *George Fox's Attitude Toward War.* Richmond, IN: Friends United Press, 1984 rev. ed.

Kauffman, Donald D., *The Tax Dilemma: Praying for Peace, Paying for War.* Scottdale, PA: Herald Press, 1978.

Kauffman, Donald D., *What Belongs to Caesar?* Scottdale, PA: Herald Press, 1969.

Kenworthy, Leonard S. *The Friends Peace Testimony.* Richmond, IN: Friends United Press, 1975.

Kraybill, Donald B., *Facing Nuclear War.* Scottdale, PA: Herald Press, 1982.

Lasserre, Jean, *War and the Gospel.* Scottdale, PA: Herald Press, 1962.

Lind, Millard C., *Yahweh Is a Warrior.* Scottdale, PA: Herald Press, 1980.

Littell, Franklin H., *The Origins of Sectarian Protestantism.* New York: Manmillan Co., 1958, 1964.

MacMaster, Richard K., Horst, Samuel L., and Ulle, Robert F., *Conscience in Crisis: Mennonites and Other Peace Churches in America, 1739-1789.* Scottdale, PA: Herald Press, 1979.

Macgregor, G.H.C., *The New Testament Basis of Pacifism.* Nyack, NY: Fellowship of Reconciliation, 1936.

McSorley, Richard, *New Testament Basis of Peacemaking.* Scottdale, PA: Herald Press, 1979, 1985.

Macy, Howard R., *The Shalom of God.* Richmond, IN: Friends United Press, n.d.

Myers, William A., *Replacing the Warrior.* Pendle Hill Pamphlet, 1985.

Mendl, Wolf, *Prophets and Reconcilers.* London: Friends Home Service Committee, 1974.

Orr, W.E., *The Quakers in Peace and War, 1920-1967.* Sussex: W.J. Offord and Son, 1974.

Palmer, T. Vail, Jr. "The Peace Testimony: Does Christian Commitment Make a Difference?" *Quaker Religious Thought* 6 (Spring, 1964).

Sappington, Roger E., *Brethren Social Policy, 1908-1958.* Elgin, IL: Brethren Press, 1961.

Schrag, Martin and Stoner, John K., *The Ministry of Reconciliation.* Nappanee, IN: Evangel Press, 1973.

Shelly, Maynard, *New Call for Peacemakers.* Newton, KS: Faith and Life Press, 1979.

Sharp, Gene, *The Politics of Nonviolent Action.* Boston: Porter Sargent Publishers, 1973.

Sider, Ronald J., *Christ and Violence.* Scottdale, PA: Herald Press, 1979.

Sider, Ronald J. and Taylor, Richard K., *Nuclear Holocaust and Christian Hope.* Downers Grove, IL: InterVarsity Press, 1982.

Snow, Michael. *Christian Pacifism: Fruit of the Narrow Way.* Richmond, IN: Friends United Press, 1982.

Snyder, C. Arnold, *The Relevance of Anabaptist Nonviolence for Nicaragua Today.* Akron, PA: Mennonite Central Committee, Peace Section, 1984.

Swomley, John M., *The Politics of Liberation.* Elgin, IL: Brethren Press, 1984.

Tatum, Lyle, ed. *The Peace Testimony of Friends in the 20th Century.* Philadelphia: Friends Coordinating Committee on Peace, 1967.

Trocmé, André, *Jesus and the Nonviolent Revolution.* Scottdale, PA: Herald Press, 1974

Wallis, Jim, *Agenda for Biblical People*. New York: Harper & Row, 1976.

Wallis, Jim, *The Call to Conversion*. San Francisco: Harper & Row, 1981.

Yarrow, C.H. Mike, *Quaker Experiences in International Conciliation*. New Haven: Yale Univ. Press, 1978.

Yoder, John Howard, *He Came Preaching Peace*. Scottdale, PA: Herald Press, 1985.

Yoder, John Howard, *Nevertheless: A Meditation on the Varieties and Shortcomings of Religious Pacifism*. Scottdale, PA: Herald Press, 1972.

Yoder, John Howard, *The Original Revolution: Essays on Christian Pacifism*. Scottdale, PA: Herald Press, 1971.

Yoder, John Howard, *The Politics of Jesus*. Grand Rapids, MI: Eerdmans Pub., 1972.

Yoder, John Howard, *What Would You Do?* Scottdale, PA: Herald Press, 1983.

Zuck, Lowell H., *Christianity and Revolution: Radical Christian Testimonies 1520-1650*. Philadelphia: Temple Univ. Press, 1975.

Index

Scriptural References

Genesis, *1:31*, 63; *12:1*, 67; *50:20*, 123
Exodus, 65
Leviticus, *10:9*, 66
Joshua, 66
Judges, *Chs. 7 and 8*, 66
Ruth, 67
Psalm, *85:10*, 68, 97
Isaiah, *1:16−17*, 178; *10:1−2*, 178; *10:5*, 122; *11:6*, 67; *31:1*, 65
Jeremiah, *6:14*, 104
Daniel, 91
Jonah, 61, 81-82; *4:6−11*, 67; *4:3*, 67
Micah, *4:3*, 67
Matthew, *3:2*, 121; *5:9*, 72; *5:39*, 44, 55; *5:43−48*, 72; *7:12*, 163; *7:24−25*, 74-75; *10:35−38*, 139; *16:4*, 81; *18:14*, 22, 35, 143; *18:15−19*, 9, 10, 142; *22:37−40*, 75; *25:45*, 99; *26:52*, 22, 163; *28:19−20*, 179
Mark, *8:34−35*, 71; *10:42−45*, 129, 127; *12:17*, 168; *13:12*, 82
Luke, *1:52−53*, 101; *4:18*, 92; *4:18−19*, 99; *6:27−28*, 161; *19:41*, 81
John, *1:9*, 45; *3:16*, 69; *3:17*, 69; *5:16−17*, 69; *14:27*, 68; *18:36*, 54; *20:19*, 133

Acts, *5:28*, 21; *5:29*, 162, 168; *10:36*, 68, 139
Romans, *8:18−21*, 94-95; *8:38*, 119; *12:9*, 124; *12:16*, 133; *12:21*, 44, 55, 124; 13, *115−116*, 123, 146; *13:1*, 76, 122; *13:1−9*, 124; *13:7−8*, 123, 146, 147
1 Corinthians, *1:23*, 72; *1:27*, 99; 7, 138; *13:8*, 147, 148; *13:12−13*, 82
2 Corinthians *5:7*, 82; *5:17*, 140; *10:5*, 21; *12:9*, 150
Galatians *3:28*, 104, 138; *4:19*, 70; *5:16*, 24; *6:22*, 110
Ephesians, *2:14*, 68; *2:17*, 133; *3:7−10*, 128; *4:3*, 47; *4:11*, 137; *4:25−27*, 142; 5:2, 71; *5:21−6:9*, 137; *6:12*, 116; *6:15*, 68, 139
Colossians, *1:15−17*, 117; *2:13−15*, 125; *2:15*, 177
Hebrews, *11:8*, 82; *12:2*, 71
1 Peter, *2:13*, 21; *2:14*, 21; *2:17*, 117; *2:21*, 42; *2:23*, 48; *4:1*, 71
1 John, *2:6*, 70; *2:15*, 64; *4:18*, 90, 150
Revelation, 45, 91; *Ch. 13*, 116; *13:1*, 119; *13:2*, 119; *13:4*, 119